The Rules
for the
Gender of French Nouns

Why your arm is masculine
but your leg is feminine,
and other mysteries
of the French language

Revised Fourth Edition

S<small>AUL</small> H. R<small>OSENTHAL</small>

The Rules for the Gender of French Nouns: Revised Fourth Edition

Published by Wheatmark®
610 East Delano Street, Suite 104, Tucson, Arizona 85705 U.S.A.
www.wheatmark.com

ISBN: 978-1-60494-306-1
LCCN: 2009928724

ACKNOWLEDGEMENTS

I would especially like to thank Catherine Ostrow who sent me many new examples (and exceptions) and Edward Paolella who sent me a constant stream of suggestions, examples, and ideas, including even ideas for entire new chapters. Numerous other readers have made additional individual suggestions.

My daughter Sadie, and many of my French friends, have been very patient with my many questions, and my wife Cindy has graciously put up with my many hours spent working on this book.

TABLE OF CONTENTS

Feminine Noun Endings

Mixed Noun Endings

INTRODUCTION

Do you wonder why an arm is masculine while a leg is feminine? Why your sofa is masculine but your chair is feminine? Does it make any sense to you that an eye is masculine, but an ear is feminine? And why should a person or victim always be feminine, even if the person or the victim you're referring to happens to be a man? And can you believe that *masculinité* is feminine!

The illogic of French gender can be puzzling and frustrating to the new student of French. Native French speakers learn the language with their mother's milk. They know automatically whether a noun is masculine or feminine, but they have no idea why. They accept the gender and take it for granted, but usually they are unaware that there are rules for masculinity and femininity that can be discovered by observation.

When, for example, I have told French friends that all nouns ending in ET, like *ballet* and *ticket*, are masculine, they are not aware of it. They will run several more ET words through their heads to verify, and then nod and say something like, "You're right, that's very interesting. I never realized it!" It's not something they are normally conscious of.

If you are a student of French who is looking for an easy way to recognize at a glance if a noun is masculine or feminine, this book is for you. In fact, even if you are a teacher of French looking for rules which will help your students, this is for you.

The rules you will find here are pragmatic, empirical rules. They were derived through my encounters with hundreds, if not thousands, of nouns from my everyday conversations and from ordinary reading.

My goal throughout has been to make sense out of the big jumble of masculine and feminine words you will run into. I'll try to present simple, easy-to-recognize, and easy-to-follow rules for you.

As we discuss each type of noun ending in the text, I'll include examples of nouns with this noun ending to illustrate it. I've done this for two reasons. The first reason is so that you can see how common (or uncommon) the noun ending is, and the second reason is to make it easier for you to recognize the noun ending pattern when you see or hear it.

For instance, if I just stated that nouns with ET endings were masculine, the rule wouldn't be connected to anything tangible and would be easy to forget. However if I tie it to examples of masculine nouns ending in ET (like *ticket, billet, valet, crochet, mollet, brevet* and *ballet)* you'll have a visual image of it and you'll be much less likely to forget it.

Because these words have been collected randomly from everyday usage, I don't make any claim that I've collected all the nouns for any noun ending, or that the lists of exceptions are exhaustive. If I have presented one exception to a rule, you may enjoy hunting for others that I have not encountered.

Indeed, my goal, and the point of this book, has never been to try to be <u>exhaustive</u> in terms of finding all the odd little exceptions, but rather to give you broad rules that are readily remembered, and that are therefore useful to you on a daily basis.

On the other hand, I **have** tried to be <u>comprehensive</u>. While other lists of rules of gender just give a few miscellaneous rules and leave you at a loss for all the rest of the nouns in the language, I've tried to give you useful rules for all, or almost all, of the nouns you will encounter.

After reading this book, if you see words like *croisement*, or *pays*, or *vin*, or *chocolat*, you will **know** that they are masculine, and, in the same way, you will recognize immediately that *ville, facture, maladie* and *essence* are feminine words. You will even know why the United States is masculine but France is *La France.*

I discovered these rules in a pragmatic and practical way and <u>it will help you to understand this book if you know how I arrived at them</u>:

My first step was to make lists of different noun endings that I encountered. Then, as I found each new noun, I wrote it alongside the appropriate noun ending in one of two columns, according to whether it was masculine or feminine.

It soon became clear that there were certain noun endings which always (or almost always) indicated that the noun was masculine. There were other noun endings which always (or almost always) indicated that the noun was feminine. I also found that there was a third, actually smaller, group of noun endings which did not follow either rule. Nouns with these endings could be either masculine or feminine.

I also found that it didn't matter if the nouns were in proper French or were in casual language or in slang. If they were in any kind of French, they followed the rules.

There followed the task of finding patterns---of organizing this myriad of masculine, feminine, and undefined endings into clear word groups that made sense, which could be considered unified rules, and were easy to memorize.

As we discuss each rule, I'll show you how it was discovered, piece by piece, and how observations were empirically grouped together to make a general rule. I'll give you examples of the nouns I found which led me to the rule.

Sometimes, when an ending is very common, I will just tell you that there are many, many more examples of this ending. At other times, an ending may be relatively rare and I'll give you all the examples I've found. Finally, I'll give you a clear statement of the rule we have just derived for your easy memorization.

After having gone through the steps of discovery with me, I hope that you will find the rules to be obvious and to make good sense, and I hope that you will have already learned each rule by the time you come to memorize it.

I've created an Appendix with a list of all the rules so that you will have them all in one place. I've also prepared an Index of all the noun endings I've mentioned and where you will find each of them discussed in the book. This should be useful as a reference for you.

For each edition of this book, as new examples and counterexamples have emerged, I have made small changes to perfect the rules, adding or modfifying as the case may have been. The sole goal has been to make the rules as accurate and as easy to use as possible.

Writing this book has been a labor of love for me. It has been constantly exciting to encounter an interesting new noun to be used as an example or as an exception, and to figure out how the nouns could best be divided into coherent groups that would be easy to memorize. I suspect that I will never feel that the work is truly completed and I'm sure that I will continue the investigation even after this edition of the book is published. I invite you to do the same.

Masculine Noun Endings

RULE ONE

T

In this section I'll take you through the steps I followed to construct our rules. The rules will make much more sense to you that way instead of just being stated as a summary.

To begin with, in looking over my noun lists, I found that all the nouns I had collected which ended in ET were masculine. Here are some examples:

*Nouns ending in **ET**:*   *creuset sommet signet brevet guichet hoquet ticket ballet billet crochet maillet mollet déchet lacet valet bonnet toupet poignet bluet porcelet signet fouet juillet calumet loquet bosquet préfet piolet piquet cabaret cadet cabinet trajet*

There are, of course, many others, which you can add at leisure. To my surprise, I found **no exceptions**---no ET words that were feminine! I was thus able to make my first small observation:

Nouns ending in ET are masculine.

I noticed that I also had collected a lot of nouns ending in AT. Here are some examples:

Nouns ending in AT: *pugilat rat chocolat éclat carat état chat odorat avocat achat contrat mandat cancrelat combat émirat malfrat climat forçat constat doctorat lectorat partenariat grabat plat*

They also all turned out to be masculine. I came upon **no exceptions** here either. Clearly:

Nouns ending in ET and AT are masculine.

I was intrigued and began to look for a pattern. Since ET and AT were masculine, I was curious whether nouns ending with IT, OT and UT would follow the same rule. Indeed, I found that nouns ending with OT, UT and IT were also masculine. Here are some of the words that I found:

Nouns ending in OT: *bibelot ergot cahot calot culot boulot ballot magot rabot capot tricot pot sot chariot flot pavot rafiot lot cachot chiot complot lingot turbot pivot cageot caillot manchot falot (exception: la dot)*

Nouns ending in UT: *statut raffut assaut but tribut début salut substitut défaut bout rajout statut*

*Nouns ending in **IT**:*   *lit bruit enduit esprit biscuit minuit crédit forfait bandit écrit dépit circuit réduit conflit déficit trait fait forfait manuscrit (exception: la nuit)*

You can see that exceptions seem to be very rare.

There is a subgroup of nouns ending in IT which are recognizable separately, because they have a different sound. These are the OIT endings. They, too, are masculine.

Here are some examples of OIT words:

*Nouns ending in **OIT**:*   *toit exploit endroit droit*

You will see later on that is the spelling that prevails. It is the IT ending, not the sound, that makes it masculine. We will discover that while nouns ending in OIR, OIS and OI are also masculine, those ending in OIE and OIX are feminine, although they all sound the same.

I also found a small number of words ending with ÂT, ÔT, ÊT, ÛT and ÎT. They, also, turned out to be masculine with one exception:

*Nouns ending in **ÂT, ÔT, ÊT, ÛT** and **ÎT**:*   *dégoût goût août fût affût intérêt prêt arrêt benêt mât surcroît dépôt impôt (exception: la forêt)*

We can now make a more general observation which I'll call Observation One:

Observation One

Nouns ending with a vowel followed by T (such as ET, AT, UT, OT and IT) are masculine.

This is a very powerful observation as (1) there are a great many French words ending with this pattern of a T preceded by a vowel, and (2) there are very few obvious exceptions.

Continuing on with my investigation, I found many nouns ending in MENT on my lists. In fact, there are literally hundreds of French nouns with this ending. It's commonly used to make a verb into a noun. For example, *un bâillement*, a yawn, comes from the word *bâiller*, to yawn. Similarly, *un changement*, a change, comes from *changer*, to change. But there are other nouns, such as *le firmament*, the skies, which are not related to a verb. Whatever the derivation, all except one of these hundreds of MENT words seem to be masculine. Here are some examples:

Nouns ending in **MENT:** *enterrement roulement sentiment serment bâillement aliment département changement firmament pansement versement paiement rayonnement garnement assortiment empêchement document gémissement dilatement tintement battement frottement testement hochement ravissement gouvernement croisement ciment*

traitement frôlement flottement
piment assortiment assolement

The only exception, *jument* (which means a mare or female horse), is obvious.

We can now go directly to Observation Two:

Observation Two

Nouns ending in MENT are masculine.

This also is a very useful observation as there are many applicable words and almost no exceptions.

My sucess with MENT led me to look next at more general ENT endings, and then at ANT endings as well. Nouns ending in ENT and ANT are fairly common in French. These also are masculine word endings. I found no nouns ending in ANT which were feminine and only one noun ending in ENT which was an exception. Examples:

*Nouns ending in **ANT**: versant éléphant garant battant*
suppléant mendiant aimant
émigrant tranchant piquant collant
instant assistant passant volant
gérant gant

*Nouns ending in **ENT**: patient moment argent parent*
équivalent vent incident agent
accident inconvénient président
récipient talent (exception: la dent)

We can go quickly to Observation Three.

Observation Three

Nouns ending in ANT and ENT are masculine.

The endings INT and ONT quickly followed, although they had many fewer examples:

*Nouns ending in **INT**: point joint appoint adjoint*

*Nouns ending in **ONT**: mont pont*

It's interesting that all the INT words I found are OINT words. I haven't found any with just a plain INT ending.

However, finding that all these vowel-NT endings were all masculine kept me looking. I gathered my observations of other nouns which ended with a different consonant than N before the final T.

Nouns ending in RT were fairly easy to find but others were uncommon. Nonetheless, all of them also seemed to be masculine endings.

*Nouns ending in **RT**: départ port effort rapport désert sort*
fort transport rempart short écart
apport tort transfert pivert brocart
(exceptions: part plupart mort)

*Nouns ending in **ST**: ballast compost must trust lest toast*
twist whist test est ouest

*Nouns ending in **GT**: doigt vingt*

*Nouns ending in **CT**: district contact tact tract respect suspect*
affect aspect verdict

*Nouns ending in **TT**: watt kilowatt*

*Nouns ending in **PT**: transcept concept*

Thus:

Observation Four

Nouns ending with a T preceded by any consonant appear to be masculine.

We can now make a very important summarizing rule:

Rule One

Nouns ending in T are masculine.

This is a <u>very</u> powerful rule because:

1. Nouns ending in T are very common.

2. They include word endings that you see frequently such as MENT, ANT, ENT, RT, AT and ET.

3. There are very few exceptions. That means you can comfortably guess, with good assurance, that any noun you encounter ending in a T will be a masculine word!

Important Note

For simplicity each rule is stated as an absolute. For example: "Nouns ending in T are masculine". However, you can always assume that there are a few exceptions unless I specifically state that no exceptions were found.

RULE TWO

S

Rule Two was an easier rule to arrive at. I noted that I was colllecting a fairly large number of nouns which were <u>singular</u> words but which <u>ended in an S</u>, like *dos, tapis, bras,* and *corps.*

Almost all of these words turned out to be masculine. As you will see below, there are very few exceptions. Here are some examples of these masculine nouns that end in S but are not plural:

> *IS: lacis commis cliquetis taudis compromis éboulis devis*
> *tapis pastis colis avis fouillis radis tennis débris croquis*
> *tournis tournevis maquis marquis ramassis chablis*
> *(fallen tree) paradis treillis métis pilotis buis cannabis dais*
> *(exceptions: vis souris brebis)*

> *OIS: minois pois putois mois bois (exception: fois)*

> *AIS: palais relais maïs rabais jais marais*

> *AS: haras matelas sas échalas cabas débarras embarras bras*
> *cadenas as bas tas verglas tracas fatras judas atlas canevas*

OS: *calvados dos os héros tournedos repos propos clos albatros*

US: *refus intrus laïus abus processus blocus rébus virus jus malus ictus rictus talus pardessus obus utérus thymus foetus cactus campus*

OUS: *remous burnous*

OURS: *secours discours concours parcours ours cours*

RS: *vers travers pervers tiers envers gars univers revers dévers*

NS: *contresens sens guet-apens*

ES: *blues*

ÈS: *accès décès procès progrès abcès succès grès excès fasciès*

PS: *temps corps*

TS: *puits*

DS: *poids remords fonds tréfonds*

YS: *pays lys*

LS: *pouls fils*

It seems clear that we can distill a useful general rule from this:

Rule Two

Singular nouns ending in S are masculine.

Nouns ending in S are not as common as those ending in T, but this rule will be very useful as well since:

> It refers to some fairly common noun ending patterns like IS, OS, AS, and US.

> It applies to any non-plural noun you may encounter ending with an S.

It's also easy to remember, as non-plural nouns ending in S are usually not encountered in English.

RULE THREE

C

Nouns ending in C also stood out to me as they are rare in English (like the non-plural nouns ending in S that we just examined). However, nouns ending in C are found fairly commonly in French and they all seem to be masculine:

Nouns ending in AC: hamac lac sac cognac tabac trac micmac bac armagnac sumac

Nouns ending in IC: public basilic fric alambic aspic hic flic chic cric lombric tic mastic pronostic trafic pic (mountain) pic (bird) pic (tool)

Nouns ending in RC: porc parc marc

Nouns ending in EC: échec bec mec

Nouns ending in OC: froc choc bloc broc toc Maroc escroc soc troc foc croc manioc

Nouns ending in UC: truc caoutchouc bouc suc stuc

Nouns ending in NC: banc blanc flanc tronc

Rule Three

Nouns ending in C are masculine.

No exceptions were found.

Again, there are not as many nouns ending in C as those ending in T, but they are very recognizable, and some are used frequently. This will be a useful rule.

RULE FOUR

I and Y

Two more noun endings which don't occur often in English, and therefore struck my eye, and will probably strike yours as well, are nouns ending in the vowels I and U. We'll take the letter I first:

In French, there are many nouns ending in I. Here are some of the ones I found ending in a **<u>consonant</u> followed by I**:

BI: colibri cagibi établi

CI: raccourci souci

*DI: étourdi bigoudi lundi mardi mercredi jeudi vendredi samedi
    midi (noon) Le Midi (the south of France)*

FI: défi

HI: chichi

KI: ski kaki

LI: ravioli repli aïoli brocoli

MI: *ennemi salami ami*

NI: *déni macaroni banni cannelloni infini*

PI: *scampi pipi épi képi tipi*

RI: *charivari cabri safari béribéri pari mari tri pourri canari*

SI: *moisi*

TI: *abruti démenti spaghetti yeti titi ouistiti*

WI: *kiwi*

XI: *taxi*

ZI: *zizi*

They are <u>all masculine</u> with the single exception of the noun *fourmi*. Note also that *merci* can be masculine or feminine *(le merci* is the thanks and *la merci* is the mercy).

As we start off looking at nouns ending in a **vowel followed by I,** it turns out that UI and AI words are all masculine too, although there aren't all that many examples:

Nouns ending in **UI**: *appui gui ennui*

Nouns ending in **AI**: *remblai délai essai geai vrai mai*

Now we come to the words ending in OI. In the first two editions I listed these words as exceptions, thinking that you couldn't predict whether they would be masculine or feminine. However, as more and more examples have surfaced the new examples have all been masculine. Thus the universe of OI words has become predominantly masculine, with three exceptions. You just have to remain aware that the fairly common words *loi* and *foi* are exceptions.

> *Nouns ending in* **OI**: *désarroi roi effroi convoi emploi octroi renvoi beffroi émoi aloi (exceptions foi loi paroi)*

There are a few orphan words in French ending in Y, derived from English of course. They also are <u>all masculine</u>. There aren't enough for a rule of their own so we'll tuck them in with the I endings:

> *Nouns ending in* **Y**: *whiskey sherry wallaby stand-by spray rugby jockey*

Our rule then is:

Rule Four

Nouns ending in I and Y are masculine.

RULE FIVE

U

Now, let's continue on with the nouns ending in U. Early on I had stumbled on a group of nouns ending in OU. Here are some of them:

*Nouns ending in **OU**: acajou sou clou chou trou fou verrou*
cou genou bijou voyou caillou
mildiou Pérou matou miaou sajou
kangourou pou joujou cajou filou

They all turned out to be masculine. No exceptions. So, how about EU?

*Nouns ending in **EU**: pieu feu pneu jeu peu lieu milieu enjeu*
aveu dieu adieu

There weren't as many but they were all masculine too.

There aren't any IU endings but there are plenty of nouns ending in AU. They are divided into those ending in YAU and those ending in EAU. The YAU nouns are less numerous, but they're all masculine too:

*Nouns ending in **YAU**: tuyau aloyau joyau boyau*

On the other hand there are many, many EAU words. EAU is a classic masculine ending in French but there are two exceptions that I found. There may be more.

*Nouns ending in **EAU**: renardeau pinceau pipeau escabeau vanneau traîneau lambeau faisceau chalumeau écriteau fléau cerceau château marteau chapeau taureau bureau oiseau fourneau tableau cerveau jumeau museau veau morceau tonneau manteau barreau naseau tasseau (exceptions: eau peau)*

I have even found one word ending in **RAU**, which is *sarrau*, also masculine.

By comparison, nouns ending in a consonant and U are relatively few and hard to find. Here are the ones that I encountered:

*Nouns ending in a **consonant and U**: aperçu insu tissu nu élu menu contenu vécu superflu dévolu tutu malotru sous-entendu fichu (exceptions: bru vertu tribu)*

This brings us to our next rule:

Rule Five

Nouns ending in U are masculine.

Clearly, this rule is much stronger for nouns ending with a vowel before the U than for those with a consonant. However, since nouns ending with a vowel before the U are much more common, they are what you are most likely to encounter anyway. This means that the rule will apply for most nouns you encounter with a U ending.

RULE SIX

L

As I organized my noun collection, looking for more patterns of noun endings that were masculine, I noticed that I had collected a fair number of IL words and that they were all in the masculine noun column. For example:

*Nouns ending in **IL**: persil fil chenil pistil nombril Brésil fournil profil sourcil péril fusil cil exil*

I'll present AIL, EIL, UIL and OIL words separately, because they look and sound different than other IL words. If you see *portail,* for example, you might not immediately think of it as an IL ending, but rather as an AIL ending. The same for EUIL and OUIL words, which sound even more different. In spite of the different pronounciations, <u>all</u> of these endings are masculine as well:

*Nouns ending in **AIL**: vantail chandail ail portail travail émail bail détail*

*Nouns ending in **EIL**: orteil oeil conseil soleil réveil sommeil*

*Nouns ending in **UEIL**: orgueil accueil*

*Nouns ending in **OIL**: poil gasoil*

*Nouns ending in **EUIL**: fauteuil deuil seuil treuil chevreuil*

*Nouns ending in **OUIL**: fenouil*

(By the way, it's an oddity that the words ending in U̲E̲I̲L̲ *(accueil)* are pronounced the same as those ending in E̲U̲I̲L̲ *(fauteuil)*.

Thus we can conclude:

Observation One

Nouns ending in IL are masculine.

As I was looking for a pattern, this led me to check out my other nouns ending with a vowel followed by a terminal L:

*Nouns ending in **AL**: carnaval animal étal cristal festival régal cheval Portugal bal mal local signal bocal métal nuptial*

*Nouns ending in **OL**: bol viol sol alcool entresol vol vitriol bémol*

*Nouns ending in **UL**: recul linceul tilleul calcul*

*Nouns ending in **EL**: naturel recel rappel tunnel gel appel ciel rituel matériel sel caramel cartel pixel bordel manuel antigel*

I found that they too turned out all to be masculine, which led to my second observation:

Observation Two

> **Nouns ending in AL, OL, UL, and EL are also masculine.**

I found only one word ending with a consonant and L, which was *scull*, taken from the English, and masculine as well. I could now make a general rule:

Rule Six

> **Nouns ending in L are masculine.**

No exceptions were found.

A rule such as this, with no exceptions, allows you to be very confident in assigning a gender to unfamiliar words that fit the pattern. You can be quite confident that any word ending in L will be a masculine word.

Rule Seven

D

Up until this point I had found six terminal letters that signaled that a noun was probably masculin. There were two vowels (I and U) and four consonants (T, S, C, and L). For two of the consonants (C and L) I had found no exceptions at all.

This led me to try to find additional final consonants that designated a word as masculine. The common French noun ending ARD led me to the letter D.

*Nouns ending in **ARD**: lard standard papelard mouchard dard charognard guépard vieillard veinard froussard canard bagnard léopard blizzard brouillard trouillard placard regard cafard bobard milliard hasard gaillard égard pinard maquisard froussard*

All these nouns ending in ARD turned out to be masculine so I started looking for other D endings. They were less common, but again, all masculine:

*Nouns ending in **ORD**: rebord sabord bord nord lord milord record*

*Nouns ending in **OURD**: sourd balourd*

*Nouns ending in **OND**: fond gond rond plafond bond*

*Nouns ending in **AND**: chateaubriand marchand gourmand tisserand chaland*

*Nouns ending in **IED**: pied lied*

*Nouns ending in **AUD**: réchaud cabillaud échafaud badaud salaud lourdaud*

*Nouns ending in **ID**: froid nid apartheid*

*Nouns ending in **END**: differend*

We can thus formulate Rule Seven:

Rule Seven

Nouns ending in D are masculine.

While nouns ending in D are only moderately common, this is another of the especially useful rules with **no exceptions** to worry about.

RULE EIGHT

N

Two more consonant noun endings are quite common. These are nouns ending in N and R. Let's take a look at N first.

The first group of nouns ending in N which caught my attention was those nouns ending in IN. Here are some examples:

> *Nouns ending in **IN**: écrin burin baratin machin scrutin vin marin dessin ravin jardin oursin cousin raisin destin matin coussin butin magasin pin lapin basin lopin turbin bouquin mannequin gratin (exception: fin)*

They were all masculine with one exception.

As I did in some of our earlier noun endings, I separated out AIN, OIN, and EIN endings because of different appearance and different pronounciation. Indeed when I had originally collected these words, I had even grouped them separately, as OIN nouns, for example, rather than as IN nouns. Some examples of these words follow:

*Nouns ending in **AIN**: poulain lendemain châtelain gain pain*
écrivain étain mondain vilain terrain
parrain drain (exception: main)

*Nouns ending in **OIN**: coin besoin témoin soin foin*

*Nouns ending in **OUIN**: pingouin marsouin*

*Nouns ending in **EIN**: rein sein plein frein*

Thus you can see why something as feminine as *le sein*, the breast, is masculine gender. It's because it's a noun that ends with IN.

I found that nouns with AN endings are also masculine:

*Nouns ending in **AN**: écran divan bilan roman ouragan*
chenapan boucan Iran tyran an
cardigan toboggan élan tympan plan
flan tian turban

And that EN words are as well. Actually all the EN nouns that I found ended in IEN. French often uses IEN to designate a man from a particular region or country or of a particular occupation such as *Parisien, historien* or *gardien*, but not all IEN words are of that form:

*Nouns ending in **IEN**: Parisien païen gardien historien*
comédien lien bien mathématicien
chien entretien vaurien électricien
statisticien

These nouns were also all masculine. In fact, up until now we've only had one feminine exception in words ending with N.

But we come now to ON endings. Simple ON endings are really quite common, probably more common than the other N endings, and they are masculine as well. However, as you will see a little further on, the group of ON endings is more complicated than any group of endings we've dealt with so far.

Nouns ending in **ON**: *toron jupon melon moellon piton menton talon blason fripon rayon maçon violon cochon béton tronçon chaton piston boulon bouton flocon lion pinson potiron pavillon blouson guidon quignon jeton poison poisson Japon ourson ton citron oignon patron graillon poinçon faon tison perron poivron pinçon bourgeon ponton étalon*
(feminine exceptions: chanson façon leçon)

We can conclude that nouns ending with a simple ON are clearly masculine.

However, now we come to our <u>first big surprise</u>, the nouns with AIS in front of the ON, and thus ending in AISON. These nouns are common, and they're <u>all feminine</u>!!!

*Feminine nouns ending in **AISON**: combinaison crevaison
cargaison maison saison
démangeaison raison terminaison
inclinaison comparaison liaison
frondaison oraison déclinaison
floraison flottaison salaison
pendaison*

Discovering that these AISON words were feminine led me to look at similar endings while preparing the current edition of this book. I discovered that OISON, the more general ISON, and even ISSON words, all also tended to be <u>feminine</u>.

*Feminine nouns ending in **ISON**: prison trahison cloison
guérison*

*Feminine nouns ending in **OISON**: cloison pâmoison foison*

*Feminine nouns ending in **ISSON**: moisson boisson cuisson*

For these three endings I have found four exceptions which are masculine: *tison, poison, frisson* and *poisson*

It would make sense to think of ISON and ISSON as the basic feminine endings and (A)ISON, (O)ISON, and (O)ISSON as subgroups, but since AISON is so common, it's difficult not to discuss it separately.

————————————

There is another group of ON nouns, those ending in ION, which is also different. These nouns, ending in **TION, SION, GION, NION, CION** and **XION,** are <u>another surprise</u>. They are also <u>feminine</u>. As they are an extensive group, we will discuss them further under Feminine Nouns in Chapter Sixteen.

We can now go on to Rule Eight:

Rule Eight

> **Nouns ending in N are masculine**
> **with the exception of those ending**
> **in ION, ISON and ISSON, all of which**
> **tend to be feminine.**
>
> **Note especially that the common**
> **endings TION, SION and AISON are**
> **almost always feminine.**

This rule that most nouns ending in N are masculine is important because there are so many nouns that end in N. It is important however to keep in mind that nouns ending in AISON and ION especially are feminine, and to remember and learn the few additional exceptions.

RULE NINE

R

The nouns ending in R have to be divided into those ending in EUR and all the rest. Nouns ending in R are generally masculine, but those ending in EUR are another surprise. I had always thought of EUR endings as designating the **male** gender for a person performing an activity such as *acteur, skieur* or *danseur* (compared to a female designating word such as *actrice, skieuse* or *danseuse).*

Indeed, that part of my supposition turned out to be correct. EUR noun endings that refer to **someone or something that does something** are masculine. Here are some of them. There are probably hundreds more.

Masculine nouns ending in **EUR**: *passeur entraîneur*
projecteur ouvreur receleur
ascenseur armateur rédacteur
orateur ordinateur mixeur danseur
sécateur radiateur disjoncteur
imposteur voleur guetteur bateleur
coiffeur facteur acteur pêcheur
instituteur percolateur chasseur
skieur aviateur docteur éclaireur

rongeur congélateur réfrigérateur
écouteur rieur empereur diviseur
sauveur rimeur commandeur
débardeur avertisseur entremetteur
videur moteur régisseur minuteur
flotteur fondateur incubateur
fomentateur rédacteur interlocuteur
bosseur admirateur etc.

They are all masculine. The surprise comes in that **the rest** of the EUR words, those EUR words that **do not** refer to someone or something that does something, are **feminine** with few exceptions.

These feminine nouns ending in EUR generally refer to a **feeling** (modesty, horror, candor, fear), to a **concept** (width, length, height, value, heat, coldness, freshness), or to a **thing** (a rumor, a flower, a tumor). You <u>don't</u> have to memorize these topics, by the way. I'm just giving them to you so you can contrast them with the masculine nouns ending in EUR. All you really need to know is that <u>if the noun doesn't refer to a person or thing that does something, it's probably feminine</u>.

*Feminine nouns ending in **EUR**: vapeur tiédeur rousseur*
ampleur tumeur ardeur valeur sueur
soeur lueur pesanteur erreur douleur
peur fleur largeur longueur humeur
candeur pudeur horreur faveur
terreur saveur stupeur grandeur
odeur flaveur moiteur grosseur
douceur hauteur rigueur rumeur
chaleur froideur profondeur liqueur
hauteur senteur blancheur rougeur

fraîcheur

*(masculine exceptions: bonheur and
malheur, intérieur and extérieur,
équateur coeur honneur)*

Thus, the big surprise for me was that, while most nouns
ending in R were masculine as expected, the nouns ending in
EUR, which I had thought of as typically masculine endings,
were half feminine.

Now, lets look at the rest of the R endings, which all turn out
to be masculine:

Nouns ending in OR: castor butor alligator trésor mirador or

*Nouns ending in AR: char bar car hangar radar avatar sonar
canular*

Nouns ending in UR: fémur dur mur futur

*Nouns ending in OUR: tambour amour jour pour four
détour vautour pourtour flour tour
(excursion) demi-tour séjour retour
(exceptions: cour tour [tower])*

*Nouns ending in ER: loyer dîner souper boucher pêcher
conseiller fer oreiller cancer toucher
déjeuner rocher danger bunker
passager archer revolver reporter
(exception: mer)*

Nouns ending in IER: dentier dossier vivier denier râtelier sablier tisonnier voiturier fichier localier coursier poudrier pilier ouvrier baudrier sommier damier papier prunier pommier poirier citronnier mûrier cerisier jardinier métier épicier huissier collier chemisier cavalier courrier portier pénitencier pionnier trésorier évier clavier bélier charpentier romancier soulier palier braconnier greffier premier grenier beurrier

Nouns ending in IR: soupir souvenir émir plaisir désir fakir menhir

Nouns ending in OIR: fermoir accoudoir dortoir heurtoir avoir remontoir dépotoir mouchoir pouvoir lavoir savoir devoir grattoir entonnoir soir espoir désespoir réservoir rasoir étouffoir tiroir manoir couloir miroir dressoir bougeoir isoloir éteignoir mouroir butoir loir parloir bavoir présentoir pressoir

Nouns ending in AIR: air flair éclair mohair pair impair (exception: chair)

Nouns ending in YR: martyr

As you see, with all these nouns ending in R, I found only four exceptions.

While the rule for nouns ending in R has to be slightly more complicated than some of those we've had so far, it should be easy for you to remember. I am forced to construct it as a three-part rule:

Rule Nine

Nouns ending in R (with the exception of EUR) are masculine.

Nouns ending in EUR that refer to a person or thing that does something are also masculine.

The rest of the EUR nouns are feminine.

Rule Ten

Other Consonants
(B, F, G, H, K, M, P, Q, Z and X)

So far most of the nouns we have encountered ending in consonants have turned out to be masculine. There are eleven more consonants that (uncommonly) form noun endings. These are B, F, G, H, K, M, P, Q, W, Z and X.

We could guess that nouns ending in these other consonants will also be masculine but we need to verify this assumption. Since there are relatively few examples of each we can examine ten of them together:

Nouns ending in **other consonants:**

*Nouns ending in **B**: plomb aplomb pub (bar)*

*Nouns ending in **F**: adhésif dérivatif pendentif poncif esquif objectif massif canif rosbif adjectif skif sportif veuf cerf golf serf oeuf boeuf récif tarif chef nerf juif (exceptions: soif clef nef)*

*Nouns ending in **G**: poing coing sang rang étang goulag*

gag shampooing smoking building
doping parking pressing parpaing
seing joug ginseng bourg zigzag
standing (exception: tong)

*Nouns ending in **H**: flash brunch lunch luth kirsch match*
scotch almanach squash (the sport)

*Nouns ending in **K**: kapok yak bifteck steak stick stock kayak*
snack anorak derrick batik Danemark
Irak

*Nouns ending in **M**: aquarium summum pensum symposium*
album parfum géranium forum
emporiumnom maximum minimum
daim essaim thym rhum clam film
dam sébum prénom sérum album
macadam édam calcium intérim
sacrum boum (explosion) (exception:
la boum [the party])

*Nouns ending in **P**: cap rap slip clip flip camp pop coup loup*
champ top drap scoop

*Nouns ending in **Q**: coq, Iraq*

*Nouns ending in **W**: bungalow*

*Nouns ending in **Z**: riz nez fez ersatz kibboutz*

These are remarkably consistent masculine nouns. I found few feminine exceptions. *Une pub*, meaning an ad is also an exception, but it doesn't really count as it's a slang abbreviation of *une publicité* which is clearly feminine.

But, now let's check the nouns ending in X. In an earlier edition we stated that these nouns seemed to be mixed. Now that we have more examples we can take another look. We'll divide them up into those ending in EUX, those ending in OIX, and those ending in other forms of X.

We find, first of all, that those nouns ending in EUX are masculine

*Nouns ending in **EUX**: gueux morveux vieux amoureux creux moelleux*

When we look at the nouns ending in other forms of X, they are predominantly masculine as well:

*Nouns ending in **X**: lynx flux influx reflux kleenex saindoux roux (redhead) roux (sauce) courroux box (calf leather) box (stall) velux inox prix taux index faux (fake) époux crucifix larynx coccyx thorax sax sphinx six dix vingt-six soixante-dix, fax, etc*

(exceptions: perdrix paix toux chaux faux (scythe)

However, the nouns ending in OIX, although we have relatively few examples, appear to be predominantly **feminine**:

*Feminine nouns ending in **OIX**: poix voix croix noix (exception: le choix)*

We have shown earlier that nouns ending in OI, OIT, OIR and

OIS were masculine, and we'll show that those ending in OIE are feminine, in spite of all of them having basically the same pronounciation. Looking above, we now see that those ending in OIX seem also to be predominantly feminine.

We can tie all of the above consonant endings together in Rule Ten:

Rule Ten

Nouns ending in other consonants are also masculine with the exception of those ending in OIX.

Nouns ending in OIX are predominantly feminine.

Rule Eleven

O

Now that we have finished looking at nouns ending in consonants, it's time to check the remaining vowels. We have already noted that nouns ending in I and those ending in U are masculine nouns. We'll look at those ending in O next. We'll see that most of the nouns ending in O are masculine. I did find a few exceptions, with an interesting explanation:

*Nouns ending in **O**: mémento studio caraco scénario macho agio vélo porno cargo recto casino oratorio verso distinguo dodo pédalo tempo poncho écho frigo imbroglio micro fiasco zoo commando turbo tango veto kilo halo lasso igloo mécano placebo gigolo ghetto brio cacao judo loto adagio solo duo trio sombrero espéranto*

(exceptions: photo dactylo dynamo météo radio moto)

It's interesting to note that <u>all six</u> feminine exceptions *(photo, météo dactylo dynamo, moto* and *radio)* are actually abbreviated forms of longer **feminine** nouns, which explains their feminine gender: *(photographie, météorologie, radiotéléphonie, radiodiffusion, radiographie, dactylographie, motocyclette et machine dynamoélectrique).*

Rule Eleven

Nouns ending in O are masculine.

We benefit from the fact that nouns ending in O tend to be masculine in Italian and in Spanish so that imported masculin nouns ending in O like *tango, macho* and *imbroglio,* coming from these two languages, conveniently stay masculine. We will see how this differs when we consider our next vowel, A.

RULE TWELVE

A

Nouns ending in A are less clear, partly because there are fewer of them in French than of the other vowels. For a while I wasn't sure whether they actually followed any rule or whether they were mixed in gender.

I finally realized that almost all the nouns that I had found which were feminine were those (recently) imported from Italian or Spanish, in which languages A endings are feminine. Thus, if you will remember that Italian and Spanish nouns ending in A, like *pizza* and *mafia*, are feminine, you can assign a masculine gender to the rest with few exceptions:

Nouns of Italian or Spanish origin ending in A (feminine):
pizza mafia villa corrida razzia
malaria mozzarela polenta marijuana
maestria influenza guérilla sangria

Other nouns ending in A (masculine): mantra cobra aléa
piranha bouddha placenta camélia
bégonia moka koala addenda alpaga
mimosa coryza visa gala harmonica
moka magma plasma Canada

anaconda Kenya agenda mascara
panda spa sofa ténia coca koala mica
charabia cinéma paprika yoga sherpa
panorama Ouganda baklava opéra
Jura caca brouhaha baba (au rhum)

(feminine exceptions: vodka véranda
polka)

Thus we have:

Rule Twelve

Nouns ending in A are masculine,
with the exception of those imported
from Italian or Spanish.

RULE THIRTEEN

Masculine Nouns Ending in E

You may legitimately be wondering at this point where the feminine nouns are, as we have been through most of the consonants and four of the five vowels. Well, we will find most of the feminine nouns among those nouns ending in E (in one form or another). However, I found large groups of nouns ending in E which are <u>not</u> specifically feminine and which don't follow any rule. I also found some groups of nouns ending in E which are masculine.

Since we are currently in the masculine noun section, we'll look next at those nouns which turn out to be masculine, despite ending in E.

The first group that we will look at are nouns ending in AGE, which is a masculine ending. This is a very large group of words. A lot of them refer to the act of doing an action, such as *tissage* and *arrosage*. Others, like *fromage* and *orage* don't refer to a verb at all. I have given a lot of examples but there are <u>hundreds</u> more:

Nouns ending in AGE: marécage rouage outrage pelage stage gage capitonnage claquage carrelage

réglage chauffage personnage
chômage passage visage potage
branchage élevage personnage
plumage âge tissage courage
dérapage orage village sabotage
arrosage ménage garage fromage
message pavage paysage péage
blocage blindage nuage rayonnage
virage avantage ratage voisinage
sage otage gavage langage forage
bagage page (person) *assemblage*
décalage griffonnage héritage
étiquetage bordage métrage flottage
soufflage corsage bornage etc.

(exceptions: image page (of a book)
plage nage rage cage)

Nouns ending in ÈGE, although fewer in number, are similar, and almost all masculine:

Nouns ending in ÈGE: sortilège liège arpège florilège solfège
piège collège manège sacrilège siège
privilège

Since AGE and ÈGE were so firmly masculine, I thought that UGE, OGE and IGE endings might turn out to be masculine too. However these latter three endings all turned out to be mixed endings, which will be discussed later.

A third group of nouns ending in E which are masculine are those nouns ending in AIRE. That came as a surprise to me.

We have already shown that those nouns ending in AIR were masculine, and logically, or so I thought, I expected that adding the E would make AIRE words feminine. I was wrong. When AIRE nouns don't refer to a person they are overwhelmingly masculine:

*Nouns ending in **AIRE** (masculine): formulaire éventaire*
salaire sanctuaire exemplaire
dictionnaire luminaire contraire
documentaire anniversaire vestiaire
repaire inventaire frigidaire
commentaire arbitraire militaire
itinéraire ordinaire annuaire
lampadaire rosaire calcaire

(exceptions: aire affaire grammaire)

When an AIRE noun does refer to a person it generally changes sex and becomes masculine or feminine depending on the sex of the person you are talking about. In other words *Jean est le destinaire* but *Marie est la destinaire.*

*Nouns ending in **AIRE** (referring to a **person,** masc or fem):*
fonctionnaire, destinataire adversaire
partenaire parlementaire libraire
militaire commissaire

The noun *émissaire* is an exception and keeps its masculine gender even if you are talking about a woman.

Nouns ending with a simple IRE also seem to be masculine.

*Nouns ending in **IRE**: sbire cachemire empire rire navire maire sourire sire délire...*
(exception: tirelire)

Another large group of nouns ending in E which are masculine are those ending in SME. Most end in ISME but some end in ASME or OSME and one ends in YSME. I'm giving you a small sample here to show the variety of these words. They are **all** masculine. There are **no exceptions**.

*Nouns ending in **ISME**: rhumatisme optimisme capitalisme formalisme organisme euphémisme égoïsme paganisme cyclisme communisme pessimisme mysticisme civisme socialisme radicalisme snobisme nudisme tourisme vandalisme alpinisme cubisme modernisme séisme intégrisme charisme mécanisme truisme professionnalisme strabisme botulisme nationalisme népotisme étatisme favoritisme laconisme etc*

*Nouns ending in **ASME**: fantasme sarcasme enthousiasme marasme pléonasme spasme orgasme*

*Nouns ending in **OSME**: macrocosme microcosme*

*Nouns ending in **YSME**: paroxysme*

An important note with regard to ISME endings is that the

corresponding **ISTE** nouns that refer to a person, such as *cycliste, communiste, socialiste, cubiste, alpiniste, pianiste, flûtiste nationaliste botaniste nudiste, touriste, humoriste, intégriste, dentiste, pigiste* and *ironiste*, are masculine or feminine depending on who is being described. (*Pierre* est *un cycliste, Marie* est *une* cycliste). Other STE endings like *liste* and *reste* are mixed.

Since ISME and ASME were masculine, I looked at other nouns ending with ME to see if I could discern a pattern. I did find two small groups of words ending in THME and GME, which seem to masculine as well.

*Nouns ending in **THME**: rythme asthme isthme*

*Nouns ending in **GME**: flegme paradigme borborygme*
(exception: enigme)

A reader also kindly alerted me to the NYME words. The words in this small group are all masculine:

*Nouns ending in **NYME**: synonyme antonyme homonyme acronyme*

This does not hold however for all nouns ending in a consonant and ME. Other nouns which end in a consonant and ME are feminine or mixed.

There is a small group of nouns ending in BLE, CLE and PLE which seems to be masculine as well:

*Nouns ending in **CLE**: obstacle habitacle socle spectacle oracle* *cercle miracle muscle siècle oncle article pinacle (exceptions: débâcle boucle)*

*Nouns ending in **BLE**: meuble immeuble tremble crible diable sable ensemble imperméable trouble double fusible visible possible câble comble râble ensemble érable portable (exceptions: cible fable table étable)*

*Nouns ending in **PLE**: périple peuple exemple simple multiple triple quadruple quintuple steeple couple*

Together these three endings (BLE, CLE and PLE) make an odd little group as other nouns ending in LE (such as GLE and FLE) are not necessarily masculine. (See Chapter 37).

There is another odd little group of masculine nouns ending with E, those ending in CTE, HTE, PTE and XTE. They are a small group but almost all masculine.

*Nouns ending in **CTE, HTE, MTE, PTE,** and **XTE**: acte entracte pacte insecte dialecte aphte comte vicomte compte mécompte décompte texte prétexte contexte (exception: secte)*

One more odd little group are the nouns ending in ZE and XE. Most of the words I came across ending in ZE are number words (as in: *le quinze mai).* The number words, at least, were all masculine.

> *Nouns ending in ZE: onze douze treize quatorze quinze seize*
> *bonze (exception: gaze bronze)*

I have found seven masculine XE words and just three feminine exceptions. I felt that this warrants XE being placed at least tentatively with the masculine endings.

> *Nouns ending in XE: préfixe fixe paradoxe saxe axe complexe*
> *réflexe (exceptions: rixe taxe annexe)*

Finally we have the TYPE endings. It's a small group but they are also masculine.

> *Nouns ending in TYPE: type stéréotype daguerréotype*

We'll combine all of the masculine nouns ending in E together in one rule:

Rule Thirteen

The following noun endings are masculine, in spite of ending in E:

AGE and ÈGE
IRE (IRE and AIRE)
SME (ISME, ASME, OSME, YSME)
Other ME endings: THME, GME and NYME
CLE, BLE and PLE

CTE, HTE, PTE and XTE
TYPE
XE and ZE

It's important to remain aware of these masculine noun endings to avoid mistakenly assigning a feminine gender to all nouns ending in E. Some of these endings are relatively common and important. They include AGE and ÈGE, AIRE and IRE, ISME and ASME, and CLE and BLE.

I think that your best bet for learning them is not to try to memorize all of them (I would memorize just ISME, ASME, AGE and ÈGE), but to look back over the examples and to learn common words as reminders such as *un insecte, mon compte, le contexte, mon oncle, le peuple, je vais faire mon possible,* etc.

RULE FOURTEEN

É

Nouns ending in É are masculine with the exception of those ending in TÉ and IÉ:

Nouns ending in É: fiancé exposé succédané combiné obsédé préposé passé imprimé énoncé café canapé relevé barbelé défilé dégonflé gré degré pré lettré conjuré avoué roué cliché péché marché négligé débraillé tracé démêlé gué sacré dérivé libéré accusé (exception: acné)

Nouns ending in **TÉ** are quite common. They are feminine and will be treated in chapter Twenty-Five when we come to feminine nouns.

Nouns those ending in **IÉ** are relatively rare. They are mixed and cannot be predicted (see Rule Twenty-One).

Rule Fourteen

Nouns ending in É are masculine,
(with the exception of those ending in
IÉ and TÉ).

Nouns ending in TÉ are feminine,
while those ending in IÉ are mixed.

RULE FIFTEEN

Compound Nouns

We now approach the end of our rules for masculine nouns. I thought of presenting this rule after the feminine nouns as I only discovered it because of some odd exceptions to feminine rules. It really makes more sense though to group it here with other rules for masculine nouns.

In organizing my feminine nouns, I noted that certain nouns such as *pare-brise* (windshield) and *parapluie* (umbrella), which have extremely feminine noun endings, are masculine. *Brise* and *pluie* are feminine. Why not *pare-brise* and *parapluie?*

I then realized that these were both compound words in which the first part of the word, PARE or PARA, refers to blocking or preventing the second half, *brise* or *pluie*. (The verb *parer* means to ward off a danger or parry a threat).

With a little research in the dictionary, I discovered that all compound nouns which started with PARE or PARA, and which referred to protection against something, were masculine. This was irrespective of whether the **noun ending** was masculine or feminine.

60

Most of these compound nouns started with PARE, and were hyphenated, but a smaller number started with the unhyphenated prefix PARA.

Masculine compound nouns referring to blocking something:

> *starting with **PARE**: pare-avalanche pare-balles pare-boue pare-brise pare-chocs pare-douche pare-étincelles pare-feu pare-fumée pare-soleil*

> *starting with **PARA**: parachute parapluie paravent parasol parapente parafoudre paragrêle*

Again, these are all masculine, irrespective of the ending.

It is important realize, however, that this only applies to those compound nouns beginning with PARA which refer to blocking or protecting against something. Other compound nouns beginning with PARA that have other meanings (usually something like: alongside of, additional), such as *parapharmacie, paralittérature* and *parathyroïde,* are assigned gender in the normal way, according to the word ending.

Since compound words referring to blocking or preventing were all masculine, I looked next at those which started with ANTI, and meant "against" or "opposed to". Since the meaning was somewhat similar, I thought they might follow the same rule. Here are some examples. They were, indeed, all masculine with just two exceptions that I was able to find.

> *Masculine compound nouns starting with **ANTI**: anticorps anticyclone antidépresseur antidote antigel antigène antihistaminique antimite*

antiseptique antivol antiradar antivirus antisérum antiskating antispasmodique antistatique anti-acide anti-inflammatoire (exceptions: antitoxine antisepsie)

Note that other nouns beginning in *anti*, in which *anti* doesn't mean "against" (such as *antichambre* and *antiquité),* follow the gender of the noun ending in the normal way.

Compound nouns starting with GARDE, which also have the same kind of meaning (to guard against), also are almost all masculine, irrespective of the ending. (*Garde* itself is also masculine).

Masculine Compound nouns starting with **GARDE***: garde-à-vous garde-boeuf garde-boue garde-chasse garde-chiourme garde-corps garde-feu garde-fou garde-frein garde-côte garde-ligne garde-magasin garde-malade garde-manger garde-magasin garde-meuble garde-mite garde-pêche garde- place garde-port garde-rivière garde-voie garde-vue (exception: garde-robe)*

Garde-malade and *garde-barrière* are masculine or feminine depending on who they refer to. In other words: <u>*Pierre*</u> *est* <u>un</u> *garde-malade*, but <u>*Marie*</u> *est* <u>une</u> *garde-malade*.

At first I had thought that it was only compound nouns which referred to protection, blocking or being against that were all male, but then I looked at nouns beginning with the prefix

PORTE, meaning to carry or contain. There are alot of them. To my surprise they too all turned out to be masculine:

Masculine compound nouns starting with **PORTE**:
porte-affiche porte-aiguille porte-aiguilles porte-allumettes porte-amarre porte-avions porte-bouteilles porte-copie porte-jupe porte-monnaie porte-musique porte-serviette porte-à-porte porte-bagages porte-baïonnette porte-balai porte-bébé porte-billets porte-bombes porte-bonheur porte-malheur porte-cartes porte-chapeaux porte-cigares porte-cigarettes porte-parapluies porte-savon porte-parole porte-skis porte-clefs portefeuille portemanteau

This led to several more discoveries. They are all masculine:

Masculine compound nouns:

starting with **BRISE**: *brise-glace brise-jet brise-lames brise-tout brise-vent*

starting with **CACHE**: *cache-cache cache-col cache-nez cache-pot cache-prise cache-coeur cache-flamme cache-misère cache-poussière cache-radiateur cache-sexe*

starting with **CASSE**: *casse-cou* (dangerous place) *casse-croûte casse-dalle casse-graine casse-gueule casse-noisette casse-noix casse-pattes casse-pierre casse-pipe casse-tête*

(Note that casse-cou (person) *casse-couilles*

casse-cul and casse-pieds are m/f depending on who you are talking about.)

*starting with **ESSUIE**: essuie-glace essuie-mains essuie-meubles essuie-phare essuie-pieds essuie-tout essuie-verre*

*starting with **LANCE**: lance-flammes lance-fusées lance-grenades lance-missiles lance-pierres*

*starting with **LAVE**: lave-glace lave-linge lave-vaisselle*

*starting with **LÈCHE**: lèche-bottes lèche-vitrines*

*starting with **CHOU**: chou-fleur chou-rave (exception: choucroute)*

*starting with **DESSOUS**: dessous-de-bouteille dessous-de-bras dessous-de-plat dessous-de-table*

*starting with **DESSUS**: dessus-de-lit dessus-de-plat dessus-de-porte*

others: marque-page

There was only one feminine exception found for all of these groups of compound nouns.

I did however find that compound nouns beginning with the prefix **CONTRE** don't follow the example of ANTI and PARE but take their gender from the noun endings in the normal way with a few exceptions. Also, the very common family of compound words starting with **SOUS** take their gender in the normal way from the noun endings. For example: *la sous-classe, la sous-couche, le sous-entendu.*

Rule Fifteen

Most compound nouns are masculine, irrespective of their noun endings, especially the important groups starting with PARA, PARE, ANTI, GARDE, PORTE, CASSE, ESSUIE and others.

When we discuss the feminine nouns I won't list these compound words as exceptions when we encounter them. I'll count on you to remember that these compound nouns are masculine. I'm doing this because listing all these compound words as exceptions would just complicate the rules for no purpose.

Feminine Noun Endings

Comment on Feminine Noun Endings

One initial caution:

Our job was fairly easy with the masculine noun endings. They were usually very clear cut and many of them had few or no exceptions.

With feminine noun endings we will also find some endings that are sharply defined. However feminine noun endings are much more likely to have some subgroups that are exceptions.

It's important to realize that while, yes, **many** French nouns which end with E are feminine, **not all** nouns ending in E are feminine. Some nouns which end in E, as we have seen, are masculine, while others are mixed and follow no rule.

And, looking at it from the other direction, it's also important to remember that while **most** feminine nouns end with some form of E, **not all** do. While investigating masculine nouns we encountered some substantial groups of feminine nouns ending with consonants.

For our first rule of feminine nouns, we'll start with the groups we have already encountered which were exceptions to masculine rules. These are feminine nouns which do **not** end with E.

RULE SIXTEEN

Feminine Nouns
which Don't End in E

You'll remember that when we discussed the rule for nouns ending with N (Rule Eight), we mentioned that there is a large group of nouns which, although they end in N, were feminine. These were the nouns ending in ION and they struck me right away as these words are everywhere:

Nouns ending in SION: *pulsion expression occasion pression dépression division exclusion inclusion incision distorsion vision allusion impression tension explosion conclusion collusion collision version mission effusion illusion contusion fission lésion succession fusion*

Nouns ending in TION: *sélection présélection condamnation audition annulation option action position déflagration contravention addition location incubation exception distraction éruption*

déclaration relation jubilation
réputation population protection
illumination malédiction munition
collation ignition identification
composition préparation invention
accusation question indigestion
imputation inanition attention
manipulation inattention incantation
inauguration adjudication
préservation présomption explication
embarcation conversation
acclamation apparition protestation
évaporation considération exécution
pulsation institution, etc (There are
hundreds more)

There are many, **many** more examples of both of these common noun endings.

These nouns are all feminine. In previous editions I said that there were no masculine exceptions at all for either SION or TION, but I was corrected by a reader who found *le bastion.* Still, one exception among hundreds of words allows you to assign feminine gender with a high degree of certainty.

Some additional ION endings, while less common, appear to be feminine as well:

*Nouns ending in **GION**: religion région contagion légion*

*Nouns ending in **NION**: union réunion opinion*

*Nouns ending in **XION**: inflexion réflexion complexion*

*Nouns ending in **CION**: succion suspicion*

There were no exceptions to any of these.

On the other hand, two uncommon ION endings appear to be **masculine**(!):

> *Nouns (masculine) ending in* **PION**: *pion lampion espion champion scorpion*

> *Nouns (masculine) ending in* **LION**: *million billion trillion lion (exception: la rébellion)*

Lastly I have found three orphan words which have other ION endings. I have found only one example of each ending so there are too few to conclude anything about them. The three words are all masculine though.

> *Nouns (masculine) with other* **ION** *endings: avion camion fion*

You'll remember another, smaller group of nouns ending in N which is feminine. This is the group with nouns ending in ISON (including AISON and OISON), and those ending in ISSON (including OISSON).

The important group to remember here is the group ending in AISON. It has common words like *maison, saison* and *raison* and it's feminine with **no exceptions**:

> *Feminine nouns ending in* **AISON**: *combinaison crevaison cargaison maison saison raison inclinaison terminaison démangeaison liaison frondaison oraison déclinaison floraison pendaison*

*Feminine nouns ending in **ISON**: prison trahison cloison guérison*

*Feminine nouns ending in **OISON**: cloison pâmoison foison*

*Feminine nouns ending in **ISSON**: moisson boisson cuisson*

The only masculine exceptions I've found so far to these groups are *tison, poison, poisson* and *frisson*.

You will also remember from Rule Nine that, while nouns which end in EUR and refer to someone or something that does something, are masculine (ie. *acteur, radiateur*), the rest of the EUR words, that is the EUR words that **do not** refer to "someone or something that does something", are feminine with few exceptions:

*Feminine nouns ending in **EUR**: vapeur tiédeur rousseur ampleur tiédeur tumeur ardeur valeur sueur soeur lueur pesanteur erreur douleur peur fleur largeur longueur humeur candeur pudeur horreur faveur terreur saveur stupeur grandeur odeur flaveur moiteur grosseur douceur hauteur rigueur rumeur chaleur froideur profondeur liqueur hauteur senteur blancheur rougeur*

(exceptions [masculine]: bonheur and *malheur, intérieur* and *extérieur, équateur coeur honneur)*

We can go to our next rule now:

Rule Sixteen -
Feminine nouns not ending in E:

Nouns ending in ISON and ISSON tend to be feminine. The important group ending in <u>AI</u>SON is feminine with no exceptions.

Nouns ending in ION are feminine with the exception of the small groups ending in PION and LION.

Nouns ending in EUR, that do <u>not</u> refer to a person or a thing that does something, are feminine.

These noun endings are very important because they apply to large numbers of nouns. The TION and SION endings especially are very common. You will see them in almost every paragraph you read, and they are basically **all** feminine.

RULE SEVENTEEN

Doubled consonants followed by E

We will now look at the noun endings which everyone thinks of as classical feminine endings. I expected them to be feminine and I was not disappointed. These are LLE, SSE, TTE, and NNE. These endings are **very common** and there are many more examples than the ones I'll give you.

Let's investigate LLE first:

Nouns ending in ELLE: venelle ombrelle crécelle flanelle noctuelle coccinelle chanterelle échelle femelle semelle selle ficelle jumelle sentinelle nouvelle bretelle vaisselle cervelle mademoiselle aisselle manivelle maquerelle (exception: vermicelle)

Nouns ending in ALLE: salle dalle balle malle (exception: intervalle)

Nouns ending in ILLE: godille grisaille maille trouvaille fouille aiguille ville douille béquille

grisaille paille dépouille citrouille
fripouille ripaille canaille racaille
chenille cheville fille taille oreille
couille mitraille rocaille houille
bataille coquille lentille pastille
oseille famille cédille flottille mantille
bille escadrille (exceptions: mille
gorille bacille)

*Nouns ending in **OLLE**: girolle colle folle*

*Nouns ending in **YLLE**: sibylle*

It's very clear that LLE is a feminine ending with very few exceptions.

There is an additional exception, *portefeuille*, which I have not listed. It is one of the compound nouns we discussed in Rule Fifteen under masculine nouns. As I mentioned at that time, I won't list these compound words as exceptions under feminine nouns. This is because we have already discussed them and I'm counting on you to remember that these compound nouns are masculine. Inserting them again among exceptions to feminine rules would just complicate the rules unnecessarily.

Now to nouns ending in **SSE**:

*Nouns ending in **ESSE**: forteresse noblesse vieillesse tendresse*
tigresse promesse adresse maîtresse
paresse duchesse princesse traîtresse
finesse caresse fesse jeunesse justesse
allégresse maladresse hardiesse
politesse messe presse allégresse

bassesse gentillesse mollesse ivresse
faiblesse liesse angoisse compresse

Nouns ending in **ISSE**: *cuisse baisse pelisse Suisse esquisse*
paroisse caisse bâtisse

Nouns ending in **USSE**: *rescousse pousse frimousse trousse*
frousse mousse (moss) *hausse gousse*
rousse

(exceptions: pamplemousse mousse
[cabinboy, foam]*)*

Nouns ending in **ASSE**: *calebasse tignasse masse terrasse*
casse caisse paillasse vinasse carcasse
crevasse classe impasse passe nasse

Nouns ending in **OSSE**: *fosse bosse Écosse crosse*
(exceptions: gosse [m/f] colosse
carrosse)

Nouns ending in **YSSE**: *(exception: abysse)*

We have found a small number of exceptions but it is clear
that SSE is also a strongly feminine noun ending.

Next, nouns ending in **TTE**:

Nouns ending in **ETTE**: *estafette oubliette chaufferette*
manchette gourmette mauviette
salopette chaînette pommette violette
devinette assiette fourchette recette
dette savonnette blanquette cachette

> *motocyclette bicyclette sucette*
> *tablette disette vedette moquette*
> *miette pipette calculette manette*
> *banquette silhouette couette bette*
> *(exception: squelette)*

*Nouns ending in **ATTE**: chatte matte datte blatte latte baratte jatte natte*

*Nouns ending in **OTTE**: hotte marotte gnognotte biscotte botte sotte flotte culotte cocotte carotte motte grotte cagnotte bouillotte menotte lotte*

*Nouns ending in **UTTE**: goutte (the illness gout) goutte (a drop) butte hutte*

*Nouns ending in **ITTE**: bitte*

And finally **NNE**:

*Nouns ending in **ONNE**: dragonne lionne cochonne poltronne patronne baronne friponne rayonne colonne consonne personne*

The ONNE ending, by the way, explains why "a person" is always feminine in French, even if the person is a man.

The ENNE endings are almost all I͟ENNE endings. These are all feminine. (The only two words I found ending in ENNE by itself, were *la benne* and *le renne*. Le renne happens to be masculine).

*Nouns ending in **IENNE**: païenne chienne Parisienne*

historienne vaurienne éolienne
comédienne mathématicienne
gardienne électricienne statisticienne

Nouns ending in **ANNE**: *canne paysanne panne banne manne*

It was no surprise that these four endings (LLE, SSE, TTE and NNE) which we think of as classic feminine endings, were definitely feminine. There were just a tiny number of exceptions for the whole large group. This naturally led me to think of other double consonants followed by E. We can immediately find two more. Although they have many fewer examples they seem to be feminine as well:

Nouns ending in **FFE**: *gaffe truffe griffe greffe* (graft) *étoffe chiffe coiffe baffe*

(exception: greffe [office of the clerk of court])

Nouns ending in **PPE**: *trappe nappe frappe échoppe enveloppe grippe steppe*

After this come a couple of <u>surprises</u>.

You might consider MME to be a clearly feminine ending, especially if you think of *femme,* or the use of *Mme* as an abbreviation for *Madame.* The problem is that while you are thinking of *femme,* you also have to think of *homme.* There are about as many masculine nouns ending in MME as feminine ones. MME turns out to be a noun ending that

79

doesn't consistently follow any rule. It's the same for the RRE ending:

Nouns ending in MME:

> masculine: *dilemme parallélogramme homme électroencéphalogramme programme gramme télégramme idéogramme somme (nap)*

> feminine: *femme pomme gamme somme (sum) flamme flemme tomme gemme*

Nouns ending in RRE:

> masculine: *cimeterre tonnerre verre lierre beurre parterre*

> feminine: *bourre jarre terre serre resserre escarre guerre Angleterre bagarre pierre barre amarre erre*

Our rule is thus:

Rule Seventeen

Nouns ending in a double consonant followed by E are feminine (with the exception of MME and RRE).

Nouns ending in MME and RRE are mixed.

This rule is very important of course, as these nouns ending in double consonants followed by E stand out and are easy to recognize. They are also very, very common.

Rule Eighteen

ÉE

Another ending that we think of as a classic feminine ending is **ÉE**. In looking for nouns with ÉE endings I found that they are indeed feminine but I did find a few exceptions. (I had thought of ÉE as so firmly feminine that I was actually surprised to find any exceptions at all):

*Nouns ending in **ÉE**: virée chambrée embardée tombée tripotée nuée montée travée contrée portée visée gorgée obsédée jetée armée giboulée marée poignée bouchée buée pensée tournée conjurée goulée tranchée bouffée brassée diarrhée destinée orchidée soirée journée année matinée idée rosée lettrée mariée volée équipée virée risée flopée avancée traversée dictée associée fiancée <u>and many more</u>.*

(exceptions: lycée musée trophée mausolée)

It's an easy rule to arrive at:

Rule Eighteen

Nouns ending in ÉE are feminine.

Again, this is a noun ending which both stands out and is common. *Musée* and *lycée* are fairly common words and are exceptions worth remembering.

Note, by the way, that these feminine ÉE endings sound exactly the same as the masculine É endings we encountered in Rule Fourteen. It's the spelling, not the pronounciation, that determines (or reflects) the gender.

Rule Nineteen

EUSE, IÈRE, IENNE and TRICE

While we are looking at classic feminine noun endings, there are several noun endings which are used as the feminine counterparts to male occupations or descriptions. The masculine endings EUR, IER and IEN (*danseur, acteur, epicier, pharmacien*) have corresponding feminine endings which are **EUSE**, **TRICE**, **IÈRE**, and **IENNE** (*danseuse, actrice, epicière, pharmacienne*).

Three of these feminine endings are not only feminine for women in these jobs or with these descriptions, they also indicate femininity for other nouns with the same endings.

> *Nouns ending in **EUSE**: passeuse entraîneuse coiffeuse*
> *allumeuse ouvreuse receleuse*
> *chanteuse skieuse rieuse danseuse*
> *bateleuse liseuse menteuse bosseuse*

Remember that, when we were discussing EUR words, we noted that machines which ended in EUR were masculine. Well, we now discover that there are also machines and tools which end in EUSE. While those ending in EUR are masculine, those ending in EUSE are, of course, feminine:

83

*Machines, tools and things ending in **EUSE**: tondeuse perceuse foreuse ponceuse trieuse trayeuse essoreuse pelleteuse faucheuse veilleuse vareuse*

Thus the universe of tools and machines is divided up into masculine and feminine, like people. The masculine ones end in EUR and the feminine ones end in EUSE.

Now let's go on to the endings IÈRE and IENNE:

*Nouns ending in **IÈRE**: matière glissière carrière sablière marbrière charnière muselière coursière ornière tanière clairière visière ouvrière mentonnière infirmière trésorière épicière romancière paupière lumière rivière portière manière crinière barrière bétonnière*

(exceptions: cimetière derrière arrière)

*Nouns ending in **IENNE**: païenne chienne Parisienne historienne comédienne vaurienne éolienne mathématicienne gardienne électricienne statisticienne*

We will meet these nouns again as part of other rules. We just saw IENNE endings in Rule Seventeen among the double consonants followed by E, and we'll encounter EUSE again in Rule Twenty-Six. However, I've grouped them together here because they fit together as female counterparts of male occupational nouns, and because other nouns with the same endings are also feminine.

Nouns ending in **TRICE** also are usually female counterparts to nouns describing a male occupation or person:

Nouns ending in **TRICE**: *actrice aviatrice cantatrice factrice impératrice institutrice débitrice créditrice délatrice directrice lectrice fondatrice fomentatrice interlocutrice spéculatrice admiratrice éducatrice exécutrice*

But nouns that end in a simple ICE instead of TRICE are **not** necessarily feminine:

Nouns ending in **ICE**:

masculine: bénéfice exercice appendice service délice artifice caprice indice orifice

feminine: hélice malice matrice police épice nourrice

We can now construct our fourth feminine rule:

Rule Nineteen

Nouns with the classical feminine endings EUSE, IÈRE, IENNE and TRICE are indeed feminine.

RULE TWENTY

NCE NSE (ANCE ENCE etc)

In reviewing my lists of words I noticed that a large group of words, those ending with ANCE, all seemed to be feminine:

Nouns ending in ANCE: malveillance surveillance croyance
chance lance confiance alliance
redevance enfance assurance
ascendance connaissance bienséance
ressemblance vraisemblance France
distance nonchalance ignorance
résistance ordonnance vigilance
croissance nuisance puissance
impuissance espérance ambulance
nuance séance préséance bienséance
défaillance quittance pétulance
ambiance constance souffrance
manigance méfiance prestance
dépendance indépendance obéissance

No exceptions were found.

Since the ENCE ending is so similar I looked at it next, and again, words with this ending seemed to be feminine with just one exception.

Nouns ending in **ENCE**: *fréquence connivence insolence impudence concurrence essence diligence tangence absence déférence conférence existence innocence apparence violence conscience audience impudence incandescence cohérence incohérence adhérence incidence évidence présence La Provence (exception: silence)*

At first I had grouped just these two endings (ANCE and ENCE) together but later I came across smaller numbers of other related nouns:

Nouns ending in **ANSE**: *panse danse anse transe*

Nouns ending in **ONCE**: *once ponce ronce*

Nouns ending in **INCE**: *pince province*

Nouns ending in **ENSE**: *récompense dépense*

Nouns ending in **ONSE**: *réponse*

There aren't many of them but they are mostly feminine, with twelve feminine examples and three exceptions *(prince, sconse* and *suspense).*

I could place INCE, ENSE, and ONSE as undetermined endings (since there are so few examples), but that would just complicate your lives for no good reason since these are such miniscule groups. It makes more sense to think of the whole group of NCE and NSE endings as feminine.

Rule Twenty

Nouns with ANCE, ENCE, and other NCE and NSE endings, are feminine.

While you would have immediately suspected words ending in ETTE or ÉE to be feminine, you would probably have been less likely to assume that ANCE and ENCE words were feminine. That makes this rule especially useful. It's relatively unexpected.

We'll find this kind of little surprise with many of the feminine endings. They won't immediately strike you as necessarily feminine, but once you are aware of each of them, you can ascribe the correct gender to a whole new group of French nouns.

RULE TWENTY-ONE

IE

I found a lot of French nouns that ended in IE. Really **a lot!** I'm giving you only a sampling here. Almost all of them are feminine. Some are the specifically feminine endings of masculine words referring to a person such as *ennemi* and *ennemie, abruti* and *abrutie, étourdi* and *étourdie*. Most, however, are simply feminine words ending in IE.

*Nouns ending in **IE**:* *laie vessie ennemie abrutie étourdie poulie magie pie scie écurie taie chatterie gâterie maladie mélodie niaiserie singerie épicerie vie Tunisie Italie Russie Algérie Turquie Syrie pénurie idéologie baie inertie folie raie galerie amnistie cavalerie partie mie poésie bougie chimie lubie monarchie charpenterie trésorerie comédie furie aphasie ironie pluie fâcherie suie catégorie bouillie décennie poulie bannie mairie manie parodie éclaircie technologie,* (and lots more)

exceptions: pie incendie caddie génie
sosie brie (the cheese)

We can also consider *paye,* ending in **YE** as a variant of IE. It's also feminine.

There are also nouns ending in OIE, which sound different but follow the IE ending rule. They tend to be feminine.

*Nouns ending in **OIE**: courroie oie proie soie voie   (exception: foie)*

On the other hand, as you remember from Rule Fourteen, while most nouns ending in IE are feminine, and those ending in É alone are masculine, those ending in IÉ don't follow either rule and tend to be mixed.

*Masculine nouns ending in **IÉ**: marié allié associé*

*Feminine nouns ending in **IÉ**: amitié pitié moitié*

Thus:

Rule Twenty-One

Nouns ending with IE are feminine.

The few ending in IÉ are mixed and follow no rule.

This rule is useful because there are so many IE words and every time you meet one you can assume it's feminine.

90

RULE TWENTY-TWO

UE

After IE, I looked next at UE endings. At first I lumped all the UE endings together, but then I realized that I needed to divide them into subgroups. This is partly for easy recognition. *Rue* looks and sounds different than *roue,* and the ending of *rue* sounds much different than the ending of *bague,* or of *musique* or of *marque,* even though they all end with UE. The other reason for separating them is that they don't all follow the same rule.

Nouns ending in UE, and OUE appear to all be feminine, with just a few exceptions:

> *Nouns ending in* **UE:** *crue retenue rue vue revue recrue verrue issue banlieue lieue grue queue cohue tenue bévue*

> *Nouns ending in* **OUE:** *roue moue boue joue*

On the other hand, words ending in GUE, QUE and IQUE

appear to be mixed, and while there do seem to be more feminine words than masculine, there are enough that are masculine so that you can't count on them to follow any clear rule. You'll be safer to look them up:

*Nouns ending in **GUE**:*

> *masculine: gringue exergue pirogue bouledogue orgue*

> *feminine: dague fugue longue mangue langue bague*
> *blague fatigue drogue morgue seringue*
> *fougue ligue*

*Nouns ending in **QUE**:*

> *masculine: kiosque risque phoque masque casque disque*
> *manque chèque roque obélisque*

> *feminine: casaque laque loque equivoque banque claque*
> *planque cloque bicoque bourrasque vasque*
> *marque barque bisque époque matraque*
> *pastèque attaque toque hypothèque coque*

*Nouns ending in **IQUE**:*

> *masculine: classique moustique pique-nique Mexique*
> *diurétique pique (spade suit)*

> *feminine: mystique (mysticism) botanique brique Belgique*
> *Jamaïque musique critique (criticism)*
> *boutique réplique logique Amérique panique*
> *politique fabrique république bique pique*
> *(pike)*

masculine or feminine depending on the person: critique mystique

Rule Twenty-Two

Nouns ending with UE are feminine (with the exception of GUE and QUE).

Nouns ending in GUE and QUE are mixed.

Rule Twenty-Three

CHE

I warned you that the feminine endings would have more groups which were exceptions. As we saw in Rule Twenty-Two above, they often don't tie up into such tight groups as the masculine endings.

The next two groups of nouns we'll look at are not huge groups but they **do** tie up in nice neat bundles. We'll start with CHE, which is a common noun ending. I'm giving you some examples here but there are many more.

*Nouns ending in **CHE**: cravache brèche paluche galoche pioche bêche broche embauche filoche péniche souche sacoche marche démarche approche fourche fiche bouche moustache bûche bâche couche mèche planche escarmouche revanche vache débauche biche pêche hanche affiche poche cache tache tâche niche dimanche cruche ruche Autriche recherche mouche manche La Manche corniche torche, etc.*

*(exceptions: bravache postiche
caniche panache porche)*

Lâche is masculine or feminine depending on the person to whom it refers.

Rule Twenty-Three

Nouns ending with CHE are feminine

This is one of those happy rules which have many examples and few exceptions and thus will be especially useful to the student.

RULE TWENTY-FOUR

MPE and MBE

Another small but reliable group of feminine nouns is the group
ending in MPE or MBE:

Nouns ending in **MPE**: *tempe trempe pompe lampe rampe*
trompe crampe

Nouns ending in **MBE**: *tombe jambe bombe trombe colombe*
hécatombe (exception: limbe)

Rule Twenty-Four

**Nouns ending with MPE and MBE are
feminine**

RULE TWENTY-FIVE

TÉ

You will remember that while in Rule Fourteen we discovered that most nouns ending in É were masculine, we noted that those ending in IÉ and TÉ were exceptions. We'll now take the oportunity to examine those ending in TÉ. They are feminine:

*Nouns ending in **ITÉ**: solennité intimité velléité autorité félicité infirmité lucidité féminité impunité masculinité perpétuité entité crudité iniquité égalité fraternité témérité vanité spécialité réalité sonorité immobilité acuité obscurité excentricité fiabilité stupidité électricité sommité concavité humidité hospitalité formalité simplicité sérénité mortalité vérité rigidité ténacité sincérité rugosité irrégularité aspérité activité capacité fluidité civilité, brutalité complexité entité fatalité imbécillité immobilité obésité etc.*

*Nouns ending in **NTÉ**: volonté bonté santé*

Nouns ending in **RTÉ**: *clarté fierté liberté*

Nouns ending in **ETÉ**: *pauvreté lâcheté gaieté honnêteté malhonnêteté habileté citoyenneté pureté impureté sûreté dureté fermeté légèreté propreté*

Nouns ending in **ÉTÉ**: *société variété propriété*

Nouns ending in **LTÉ**: *difficulté*

Nouns ending in **AUTÉ**: *cruauté nouveauté beauté*

Nouns ending in **PTÉ**: *volupté*

These are **all feminine** noun endings. There were only a few masculine exceptions found for all the endings in TÉ: *aparté comité traité été velouté pâté.*

Rule Twenty-Five

Nouns ending with TÉ are overwhelmingly feminine.

Note especially the very common ending ITÉ.

The rule for TÉ endings is strong, but you need to remember the exception for the common noun *été* (summer). All four seasons are masculine, by the way.

RULE TWENTY-SIX

U-CONSONANT-E

As I collected different noun endings I found many like URE, ADE, INE, UNE, IDE, ODE, UDE and others. It was a challenge to organize them into meaningful groups.

For example, I had to decide whether it would be better to group URE with other endings starting with U (such as UDE and UNE), as a U-CONSONANT-E noun ending? Or would it be preferable to group it with ARE, IRE and ORE, as a "vowel-followed-by-RE" noun ending?

While URE, as we will see, is a common and very strong feminine ending, ARE doesn't follow any rule and IRE is masculine. In fact RE endings in general turn out to be mixed, as we'll see in Rule Thirty-Five.

Thus, URE fits better with UNE, UVE, UTE and USE which are also feminine endings. It was thus better to make our rule for U followed by a consonant and an E. The goal throughout has been to find rules for you which are as clear as possible, as easy to recall as possible, and as consistent as possible.

As I just explained, I ended up grouping U-CONSONANT-E

endings together. They are not all feminine, but enough are feminine for the grouping make good sense.

URE is a very strong feminine ending, with many, many examples and few exceptions.

*Nouns ending in **URE**: tenture mesure griffure fioriture*
souillure masure envergure filature
coiffure facture soudure ordure
injure rayure éraflure égratignure
bravoure figure rature mixture
peinture allure heure foulure
blessure enflure brûlure moisissure
fissure capture garniture levure
lecture monture brochure nature
devanture désinvolture morsure
carrure fracture préfecture
encoignure tonsure culture
floriculture denture nervure piqûre
manucure salure manufacture
rupture dorure félure ferrure
procédure

(exceptions: murmure sulfure
parjure cyanure)

On the other hand, the two words I found ending in **AURE**, *(dinosaure, centaure)* are masculine.

Other U-CONSONANT-E endings aren't seen as commonly but most are also firmly feminine:

*Nouns ending in **USE** (and **OUSE**): cause excuse intruse bouse*
blouse épouse pelouse

*Nouns ending in **EUSE**: passeuse entraîneuse coiffeuse*
allumeuse ouvreuse receleuse
chanteuse skieuse rieuse danseuse
bateleuse liseuse menteuse bosseuse
(and many more)

*Nouns ending in **UVE**: cuve épreuve veuve douve louve preuve*
(exception: fleuve fauve)

*Nouns ending in **UDE**: sollicitude béatitude chiquenaude*
servitude mansuétude étude lassitude
solitude habitude badaude lourdaude
maraude prude inquiétude quiétude
émeraude certitude multitude soude
gratitude amplitude plénitude

(exceptions: coude interlude prélude)

*Nouns ending in **UNE**: rancune lacune prune fortune faune*

*Nouns ending in **UTE**: route chute rechute croûte émeute*
meute faute brute minute culbute
(exception: doute)

*Nouns ending in **UPE**: croupe troupe taupe soupe coupe*
soucoupe jupe (exception: groupe)

The ending ULE leans towards feminine but there are enough
ULE nouns that are masculine that you can't really predict the
gender of a new ULE noun with any certitude. You can guess
feminine if you don't have access to a dictionary or you are
in conversation, but for an important paper it's safer to look
them up.

Nouns ending in **ULE***:*

> *feminine: cagoule crapule poule opuscule rotule pilule*
> *capsule spatule épaule mule gueule ampoule*
> *mandibule gaule férule fécule*

> *masculine: véhicule testicule préambule monticule pécule*
> *tentacule*

There are also a small number of endings in this U-CONSONANT-E group which actually lean toward a predominance of masculine endings. However there enough feminine endings that we have to say that they are mixed and don't consistently follow any rule. Fortunately these are uncommon endings with few examples. I'll combine them together here:

Nouns ending in **UBE, UCE, UGE** *and* **UME***:*

> *masculine: incube succube cube tube pouce grabuge*
> *ignifuge subterfuge juge chaume royaume*
> *baume volume rhume costume*

> *feminine: aube puce jauge sauge luge auge brume plume*
> *paume*

We can thus arrive at the following rule:

Rule Twenty-Six

Nouns ending in U-CONSONANT-E are predominantly feminine, but some less common subgroups are mixed.

URE, especially, is a very common noun ending and almost always feminine. If you consider the U-CONSONANT-E endings as a whole, I have found at least 150 feminine words (not counting all the rest of the EUSE words, which I haven't bothered to list and which are all feminine), and only about 30 masculine words. If you have to guess, guess feminine. If it's crucial to get it right, it's safest to look it up.

Rule Twenty-Seven

A-CONSONANT-E

Next we will tackle the A-CONSONANT-E noun endings. This is also a complicated group. You will remember from Rule Thirteen that **AGE** is a common **masculine** ending despite ending with E. The rest of the A-CONSONANT-E endings tend, however, to be feminine.

The most common of these feminine endings is ADE:

*Nouns ending in **ADE**: estrade brimade taillade arcade bourgade passade boutade mascarade brigade saccade fusillade Barbade oeillade rasade rade palissade myriade façade limonade pommade glissade muscade escalade escapade cavalcade incartade pintade bousculade esplanade (exception: stade jade grade)*

Then there is a group of other endings which are less common, but which are mostly feminine:

*Nouns ending in **ABE**: syllabe*

*Nouns ending in **ACE**: besace limace race glace trace face menace audace place espace (in printing) (exceptions: espace rapace palace)*

*Nouns ending in **AFE**: agrafe carafe girafe*

*Nouns ending in **ALE**: générale cathédrale escale cavale cale pédale rafale capitale cabale (exceptions: pétale scandale)*

*Nouns ending in **AME**: came trame rame lame réclame (exception: drame)*

*Nouns ending in **APE**: étape tape soupape chape cape*

*Nouns ending in **ATE**: plate rate date (exception: pirate)*

*Nouns ending in **AVE**: entrave cave rave épave octave lave enclave betterave*

Finally, as with the U-CONSONANT-E endings, there are also a small number of endings in this A-CONSONANT-E group which are mixed and do not follow any rule. First of these is the ending ANE:

*Nouns ending in **ANE**:*

masculine: octane organe filigrane arcane

feminine: caravane tisane liane cabane cane gentiane

There are four more fairly rare A-CONSONANT-E endings which also appear to be mixed:

Nouns ending in ASE, ARE, AZE and AKE:

masculine: vase (for flowers) phare cigare kamikaze

feminine: vase (mud) base phrase gare tiare mare gaze cake

Nouns ending in Â-CONSONANT-E (below) actually seem to lean toward being masculine but we don't have enough examples to be sure.

Nouns ending in Â-CONSONANT-E

masculine: râle mâle crâne âne châle blâme

feminine: râpe âme

We can summarize our results in our next rule:

Rule Twenty-Seven

Nouns ending in A-CONSONANT-E (with the exception of AGE) are predominantly feminine.

Nouns ending in AGE are masculine.

As with the previous rule, remember that there are small groups of nouns ending in A-CONSONANT-E that are exceptions and follow no rule.

RULE TWENTY-EIGHT

I-CONSONANT-E

We move on now to I-CONSONANT-E noun endings. As with the previous two groups that we examined, there will be deviant sub-groups which follow no rule. However, rather than dealing with each noun ending such as INE, IVE, ISE, IPE and IRE as a separate category, it makes more sense to group them together in as consistent a way as possible.

There are three endings which seem firmly feminine. These are IVE, ISE and INE. We'll start with IVE. Words ending in IVE are all feminine:

*Nouns ending in **IVE**: dérive olive tentative gencive lessive sportive salive esquive rive juive endive*

Next we'll look at ISE endings, as well as two ISE subgroups which we'll consider separately because they look and sound different: the OISE and AISE endings.

*Nouns ending in **ISE**: devise franchise crise reprise convoitise prise remise marquise*

> entreprise brise église valise emprise
> gourmandise friandise chemise
> métise

*Nouns ending in **OISE**:* ardoise toise framboise

*Nouns ending in **AISE**:* aise falaise braise mayonnaise chaise
> foutaise charentaise

There was only one exception found for all three of these endings. It's *le malaise.*

Nouns ending in INE, or some variation of INE, such as AINE, UINE or EINE, are fairly common. They are all feminine too, with very few exceptions found:

*Nouns ending in **INE**:* tartine glycine comptine machine
> vitrine poitrine mine piscine échine
> doctrine colline médecine origine
> sourdine caféine insuline mandoline
> margarine cabine (exception:
> pipeline)

*Nouns ending in **AINE**:* mitaine haine aine fontaine
> porcelaine plaine cheftaine laine
> mondaine dizaine douzaine vingtaine
> marraine centaine marjolaine
> mitaine (exceptions: capitaine
> domaine)

*Nouns ending in **EINE**:* veine déveine haleine peine baleine

*Nouns ending in **UINE**:* fouine bruine coquine

I found only two words ending in **OINE**. They both turned out to be masculine, (*moine, patrimoine*). Nevertheless we can say that INE words seem reliably feminine.

Thus we can safely conclude that if you encounter a noun ending in IVE, INE or ISE you can expect it to be feminine. There are very few exceptions.

However we now come to those noun endings in the I-CONSONANT-E family **which are mixed** or don't have enough examples to assign them. These are IDE, IFE, IGE, ILE, IME, IPE and ITE.

*Nouns ending in **IDE**:*

> *masculine: bolide liquide fluide fongicide insecticide vide homicide génocide bide*

> *feminine: aide (help) ride pyramide égide*

*Nouns ending in **IFE**:*

> *masculine: calife*

*Nouns ending in **IGE**:*

> *masculine: prestige vertige vestige*

> *feminine: égide neige tige*

*Nouns ending in **ILE**:*

> *masculine: volatile mobile asile domicile bile vigile fossile crocodile voile (veil)*

> *feminine: étoile voile (sail) toile aile argile île*

Nouns ending in **IME**:

    masculine: régime abîme crime millésime

    feminine: escrime rime prime frime déprime victime lime
        cime estime

Nouns ending in **IPE**:

    masculine: principe

    feminine: pipe équipe

Nouns ending in **ITE**:

    masculine: termite satellite ermite site rite granite
        graphite anthracite trilobite plébiscite mérite

    feminine: mite fuite réussite poursuite suite marmite
        conduite dynamite hépatite bronchite orbite
        appendicite

Nouns ending in **IXE**:

    masculine: préfixe fixe

    feminine: rixe

A few people-words like *guide, imbécile* and *aide* (assistant), can be either masculine or feminine depending on who you are talking about.

———————————

There are even two I-CONSONANT-E endings which appears to be **masculine noun endings**. These are IZE and IRE. We'll treat IZE first as there are only two examples, both numbers, which are of course all masculine:

*Masculine nouns ending in **IZE**: treize seize*

*Masculine nouns ending in **IRE**: sbire sire cachemire empire
rire navire maire sourire délire pire
(exception: tirelire)*

An ending which is worth discussing separately is the ending OIRE, a subgroup of the IRE endings. As OIR endings were masculine, I had assumed that OIRE endings were their feminine counterpart and that OIRE would be a feminine ending. *(la gloire,* etc.). I was surprised to find that OIRE is mixed and follows no rule:

*Masculine nouns ending in **OIRE**: prétoire réfectoire ivoire
auditoire pourboire territoire
Directoire conservatoire oratoire
interrogatoire exutoire laboratoire*

*Feminine nouns ending in **OIRE**: échappatoire pétoire victoire
baignoire mémoire passoire gloire
nageoire mâchoire histoire armoire
bouilloire foire mangeoire*

And let's not forget that AIRE, another IRE subgroup, is also a surprise masculine ending, as we saw in Rule Thirteen.

Nouns ending in AIRE which don't refer to a person are masculine.

Nouns ending in AIRE which do refer to a person, such as *libraire, fonctionnaire* or *adversaire,* generally become masculine or feminine depending on the sex of the person you are talking about.

*Masculine nouns ending in **AIRE**: formulaire éventaire sanctuaire exemplaire dictionnaire luminaire documentaire contraire anniversaire vestiaire repaire inventaire frigidaire commentaire arbitraire ordinaire militaire itinéraire annuaire lampadaire rosaire calcaire primaire (exceptions: aire affaire grammaire glaire)*

Nouns ending in ICE should also be treated separately. As you remember from Rule Nineteen, some usually represent female versions of male occupational nouns and end in TRICE. Those are all naturally feminine gender.

*Nouns ending in **TRICE**: actrice aviatrice institutrice impératrice cantatrice instructrice factrice débitrice créditrice délatrice directrice lectrice fondatrice fomentatrice rédactrice interlocutrice inspectrice*

The rest of the ICE nouns are mixed and don't follow any rule:

*Nouns ending in **ICE**:*

> *masculine: supplice appendice indice bénéfice exercice service délice artifice caprice orifice édifice sacrifice précipice dentifrice armistice vice*

> *feminine: hélice épice malice police matrice nourrice justice*

How can we make a coherent rule out of all of this??? Certainly not as easily as for some of our simpler previous rules. What follows is the best that I could do.

Rule Twenty-Eight

The I-CONSONANT-E endings are a mess.

The common endings IVE, ISE, INE, AINE, and TRICE are feminine.

IRE and AIRE are masculine!

Other I-CONSONANT-E endings, including the important endings OIRE, ICE and ITE, are mixed and follow no rule.

This is a more complicated rule to learn and certainly less helpful than some others we've encountered, but just remembering that the common endings IVE, INE, AINE and ISE are feminine may prove useful, as it also will be to remember that OIRE and ICE endings are mixed and are not always feminine.

Rule Twenty-Nine

R-CONSONANT-E

We are now coming close to the end of the feminine noun endings, but we have another fairly large feminine group: those nouns ending in R-CONSONANT-E. None of the subgroups below is very large but there are few exceptions for the entire group:

Nouns ending in RBE: *herbe superbe tourbe courbe*
(exceptions: verbe adverbe)

Nouns ending in RPE: *serpe écharpe*

Nouns ending in RME: *ferme arme forme larme alarme chiourme (exceptions: charme terme gendarme)*

Nouns ending in RNE: *lucarne baliverne lanterne berne caserne borne (exception: cerne)*

Nouns ending in RCE: *farce force écorce (exception: commerce)*

Nouns ending in RDE: gourde bourde maquisarde corde
mansarde veinarde froussarde
trouillarde garde horde

Nouns ending in RGE: cierge vierge verge serge recharge
charge marge barge gorge orge berge
courge   (exception: large)

Nouns ending in RSE: averse entorse bourse Corse course
herse (exceptions: morse inverse)

Nouns ending in RVE: réserve minerve morve verve conserve

Nouns ending in RTE: alerte perte porte escorte carte

You do have to remember that the ending RRE, which we have already found to be **mixed** back when we looked at DOUBLE CONSONANT-E endings, is also an R-CONSONANT-E ending.

The rule can thus be fairly simple:

Rule Twenty-Nine

Nouns ending in R-CONSONANT-E are mostly feminine, (with the exception of those ending in RRE).

Nouns ending in RRE are mixed.

RULE THIRTY

N-CONSONANT-E

When I had to discard the TE rule (see "Observation on TE endings" below), I was left with a group of feminine nouns, those ending in NTE, which didn't seem belong to any rule I had at the time:

Nouns ending in NTE: *patiente descente détente garante*
enceinte attente fente plante
épouvante charpente mendiante
immigrante tente assistante plainte
pointe émigrante pente honte fonte
ponte (eggs) brocante mante

There were two exceptions *mastodonte* and *ponte* (big shot). However, note that *trente*, *quarante* and *cinquante* are also exceptions as all numbers are masculine.

I looked for other N-CONSONANT-E nouns and found several more feminine endings that we had already encountered.

To start off with there were the **NNE** endings from Rule Seventeen (double consonants followed by E). They were also clearly feminine.

Next there were the **NCE** endings and the **NSE** endings which we had encountered in Rule Twenty, predominently as ANCE, ENCE and ANSE endings. These also were feminine endings.

I also found the NDE ending, which had been treated as an "orphan" ending in previous editions, without a family of its own to fit into. NDE now fit nicely into this new N-CONSONANT-E family, and was also feminine.

> *Nouns ending in **NDE**: bande plate-bande sarabande fronde demande amande réprimande amende propagande légende Irlande lande Hollande ronde tisserande blinde marchande sonde commande bonde (exceptions: monde dividende)*

I did find one ending which is mixed:

> *Nouns ending in **NGE**:*
>
> *masculine: losange ange singe challenge mensonge mélange songe échange change rechange lange linge*
>
> *feminine: rallonge éponge longe fange mésange vidange vendange orange frange*

Finally, I found three unattached little N-CONSONANT-E

words which are masculine exceptions: *genre, branle* and
chambranle.

Rule Thirty

**Nouns ending in N-CONSONANT-E are
feminine with the exception of NGE
which is mixed.**

Rule Thirty-One

VE

In collecting noun endings I came across two words with the ending LVE, which were both feminine but which didn't seem to belong to any larger grouping.

*Nouns ending in **LVE**: salve valve*

In looking for a home for them, a new pattern came to my eye. I noted that we had encountered another feminine ending, IVE, among the I-CONSONANT-E endings (Rule Twenty-Eight):

*Nouns ending in **IVE**: dérive olive tentative gencive lessive sportive salive esquive rive juive endive (exception: glaive)*

We had also encountered AVE endings among the A-CONSONANT-E noun endings (Rule 27):

*Nouns ending in **AVE**: entrave cave rave épave octave lave enclave*

These were all feminine. There were practically no exceptions. It was starting to look as if we had something here.

Then there were the feminine UVE nouns that I found among the U-CONSONANT-E endings in Rule 26:

Nouns ending in **UVE**: *cuve épreuve veuve douve louve preuve (exceptions: fleuve fauve)*

I only found one noun ending in ÔVE , but it was feminine too:

Nouns ending in **ÔVE**: *alcôve*

I looked at RVE endings among the R-CONSONANT-E endings (Rule Twenty-Nine) and I found the following nouns:

Nouns ending in **RVE**: *réserve minerve morve verve conserve*

Again, all feminine with no exceptions. This was becoming exciting! I looked further and found some more VE endings among nouns ending in ÈVE (See Rule 33):

Nouns ending in **ÈVE**: *sève crève grève relève*

These also were all feminine with no exceptions found.

Finally, for nouns ending in ÊVE, I found only one example and one exception. It's hard to say anything about this ending:

Nouns ending in **ÊVE**: *trêve (exception: rêve)*

We can safely conclude:

Rule Thirty-One

Nouns ending in VE are feminine.

This is a strong rule, with few exceptions found. Since feminine rules tend to have a lot of groups which don't fit, this is probably one of our strongest feminine rules. Thus, if you keep in mind that the fairly common noun, le rêve, is the one important exception, the rule will be very useful.

Rule Thirty-Two

GNE

Finally we come to a miscellaneous ending that doesn't fit into a larger identified group, but which is fairly large and appears to be primarily a feminine ending.

Nouns ending in **GNE**: *consigne castagne rogne charogne beigne vergogne hargne Allemagne lasagne besogne Bourgogne Bretagne compagne campagne cigogne consigne enseigne épargne Espagne ligne Gascogne montagne Pologne vigne guigne (exceptions: bagne pagne peigne cygne signe insigne)*

This will be the last of our feminine rules.

Rule Thirty-Two

Nouns ending with GNE are predominantly feminine.

RULE THIRTY-THREE

Wines, Cars, and other Categories

An odd exception that I found to some of our feminine rules was in regard to wines. The regions *La Champagne*, *La Bourgogne* and *Les Graves* are feminine, as one would expect from the noun endings. However, the wines *le champagne, le bourgogne,* and *le graves*, are masculine. As I investigated further I discovered that **almost all wines** that I encountered were masculine:

> *champagne bourgogne graves sauternes chablis bordeaux chardonnay beaujolais médoc pommard pomerol meursault pinot noir pinot gris pinot blanc merlot cabernet gewurtztraminer riesling sauvignon tokay grenache gigondas Châteauneuf-du-Pape Saint-Émilion viognier muscat muscadet sylvaner mâcon etc... exception: syrah*

I decided that the explanation was perhaps that in saying *"un bourgogne",* it is understood that one is really saying "**un vin de Bourgogne**".

This explanation turned out to be almost certainly correct. A reader kindly pointed out to me that **automobiles** are all feminine. You say <u>une</u> *Peugeot,* even though Peugeot ends with a T, and *une* diesel, even though *diesel* ends with an L. It's understood that you are referring to **une voiture** Peugeot and **une voiture** diesel. Similarly, you say *une Citroën, une Renault or une quatre chevaux* for the same reasons.

To cement the argument, a French friend then pointed out that if you are referring to a **truck**, you say *un Peugeot, un Citroën* and *un Renault*, because you are really saying *un camion Peugeot*, etc.

Similarly, if you are talking **a painting**, or **un tableau,** it's always masculine. You say *"un Monet"* of course, but also *"un Cézanne"*. The ANNE ending doesn't make it feminine because you are talking about *un tableau de Cézanne.*

And even if the artist is a woman it's *"un Mary Cassatt"* for the same reason. You are talking about *un tableau de Mary Cassatt.*

It's "Une Heineken, s'il vous plaît", for example, because **une bière** *Heineken* is understood.

In the boulangerie you ask for *"un céréale et un campagne"* although *céréale* and *campagne* are feminine words, because you are asking for **un pain** céréale et **un pain** de campagne. (*Une baguette* is feminine because *baguette* is a separate noun in its own right. It's not *"un pain de"* baguette).

Similarly, in the fromagerie, if you ask for *une* chèvre, you are asking for a female goat. Instead you ask for *un* brie et *un* petit chèvre, or you say *Je préfère* *le* brebis, because it's **fromage** that you are talking about. When you ask for *un camembert* you're really asking for *un fromage de Camembert*. (On the other hand *la Mimolette, la tomme* and *la mozzarela* have names of their own, like *une baguette)*.

In the days of steamboats one referred to *"un vapeur"*, short for *"un **bateau** à vapeur"*. Now we refer to *"une Visa"*, meaning *"une **carte** Visa"*. (A visa for a foreign country is un visa as it should be, given that it's a noun ending in an A).

Numbers, colors, trees and seasons also seem to be all masculine, but don't fit clearly into the above pattern. Let's talk about numbers first.

Numbers seem to all be masculine, even ones which clearly have feminine endings like *un mille,* and *cinquante* and *quarante.* Perhaps it's because you are referring to *le **numéro** cinquante* or *le **chiffre** cinquante,* which would help it to fit the pattern, but that's just a guess on my part. The fact that numbers are masculine however is certainly true.

Colors are odd. *Bleu, jaune, rouge, vert, gris, rose, noir, blanc, violet;* they are all masculine. Even *jaune* with the feminine ending UNE is masculine. And even the color *rose* is masculine even though the flower, *une rose,* is feminine. What makes colors odd though, is that the category, *la **couleur***, is feminine. Thus we have *un vert vif, un gris leger*, when we talk of the color itself. But, paradoxically, we talk of *la couleur verte* and *la couleur grise*, because there *verte* and *grise* are adjectives modifying *couleur.*

Trees also seem to be almost all masculine, even ones with what should be feminine endings. *Orme, saule, chêne, frêne, hêtre, acajou, pin, épicéa, érable, cerisier, merisier, pommier, prunier, figuier, etcetera,* they are all masculine with the single exception of *aubépine.* But it's not clear that the reason that trees are masculine is because **un arbre** is masculine. *(Un* *animal* is masculine but there are plenty of animal names which are feminine.)

Seasons are masculine too. *Printemps* and *hiver* are naturally masculine endings, but *été* should be a feminine ending and *automne* has no clear reason to be masculine, but that's the way it is. *(La saison* is of course feminine). **Months** are all masculine *(un septembre affreux)*. As are **days of the week** *(Il est venu le lundi* or *le dimanche)*.

We can fashion a rule which holds for a good number of general categories out of all of this.

Rule Thirty-Three

> **Wines, trees, colors, numbers, days of the week, months and seasons are masculine.**
>
> **Autos are feminine, and the genders of nouns in other categories are determined in a similar fashion when the nouns don't stand alone but are "abbreviations".**
>
> **For example when _une Renault_ means _une voiture_ Renault, or _un_ chèvre means _un fromage_ de chèvre.**

As with the compound nouns, I didn't list these words as exceptions to other rules. I will rely on you to remember this rule of categories.

Note that this **doesn't** hold for other types of categories. For example, ***un oiseau*** and *un martinet* are masculine but *une caille* and *une hirondelle* are feminine. This is because they, and the names of other birds, stand on their own and aren't short for *un oiseau caille* or *un oiseau hirondelle.*

The gender of bird names, as well as the gender of most other categories (like animals for instance), follows the noun endings.

Mixed Noun Endings

Comment on Noun Endings that Don't Follow any Rule

You may be wondering, "If nouns with these endings don't follow a rule for either masculinity or femininity, why do we have rules for them? Why not just ignore them?". However, it's important to know which words you <u>can't</u> assign a gender to automatically and that you have to look up and memorize. Otherwise there is a good chance that you might assume that they are either masculine or feminine according to their appearance or sound.

Thus, when grouping the nouns I encountered by gender, if I found a noun ending which was sometimes masculine and sometimes feminine, I felt that this was also an important bit of information. Perhaps not as important as finding a common ending which was all masculine or all feminine, but important and useful nevertheless.

I hope that you will find that knowing which noun endings are solidly mixed is one more helpful piece of information. You may decide to memorize certain of these endings and use the others just for reference, but that will be up to you.

RULE THIRTY-FOUR

È-and Ê-CONSONANT-E

Part 1- È-CONSONANT-E

I first encountered nouns from the È-CONSONANT-E group when I was looking at the common ending ÈRE, but then I continued to find other small groups of nouns ending with È-CONSONANT-E, but with different consonants. These included such endings as ÈNE, ÈME and ÈVE.

There are some È-CONSONANT-E nouns which we have already encountered under previous rules as masculine or feminine. These included **ÈGE** as a masculine noun ending (Rule Thirteen) and **IÈRE** as a feminine noun ending (Rule Nineteen).

Nonetheless, it seemed to make sense to group the rest of the È-CONSONANT-E noun endings together, as they all seemed to be mixed masculine and feminine.

Let's start with ÈRE as this is the most common ending in the group. The noun ending ÈRE is used as a feminine equivalent for the masculine occupational ending ER, as in *boucher-bouchère* and *boulanger-boulangère*. In this usage ÈRE is naturally feminine. However there are many more words with ÈRE endings, and while there are slightly more that are feminine than are masculine, there are certainly enough masculine so that you can't count on ÈRE words to follow any rule:

Nouns ending in ÈRE:

> *masculine: frère père ampère hélicoptère monastère presbytère caractère mystère cerbère réverbère débarcadère embarcadère*

> *feminine: congère patère galère bruyère artère galère bouchère boulangère passagère conseillère misère étagère colère vipère enchère sphère atmosphère commère fougère bruyère mère*

Nouns ending in ÈNE, ÈPE, ÈLE, ÈDE, ÈME, ÈSE and ÈCE have few examples, but these few examples are fairly evenly mixed between masculine and feminine nouns:

Nouns ending in ÈNE, ÈPE, ÈLE, ÈDE, ÈME, ÈSE, ÈTE and ÈCE

> *masculine: bipède remède zèle modèle problème barème système blasphème poème kérosène phénomène gène cèpe manganèse dièse diabète*

> *feminine: espèce pièce nièce pinède Suède stèle crème brème rêne sirène ébène arène scène thèse diérèse diurèse planète Crète comète*

You'll note that ÈCE so far has no masculine examples may indeed eventually turn out to be a feminine ending. However, as of yet we have too few examples to confidently assign it as a feminine ending.

Then there are three endings that we have met previously. First the masculine ending ÈGE from Rule Thirteen, and then the two feminine endings IÈRE and ÈVE from Rules Nineteen and Thirty-One.

Masculine nouns ending in ÈGE: solfège piège collège manège sacrilège siège privilège (exception: Norvège)

Feminine nouns ending in IÈRE: matière glissière charnière muselière coursière tanière clairière ornière visière infirmière épicière romancière paupière lumière rivière portière manière crinière sablière barrière (exceptions: cimetière derrière)

Feminine nouns ending in ÈVE: sève crève grève relève

Part 2- Ê-CONSONANT-E

Now we'll move on to a related noun ending, Ê-CONSONANT-E. These endings also seem to be predominantly mixed, although they have fewer examples than the È-CONSONANT-E noun endings.

Nouns ending in ÊVE, ÊNE, ÊLE and ÊME:

masculine: *rêve pêne chêne extrême crêpe (cloth) Carême* *feminine:* *trêve gêne rêne grêle crêpe* (food) *poêle*

And we finish with ÊTE which seems to be a feminine ending:

Feminine nouns ending in ÊTE: *tempête tête bête arête crête enquête*

We'll make the best rule that we can from this:

Rule Thirty-Four

Nouns ending in È-ᴄᴏɴsᴏɴᴀɴᴛ-E and Ê-ᴄᴏɴsᴏɴᴀɴᴛ-E are mixed and follow no rule (with the exception of the masculine ending ÈGE and the feminine endings IÈRE, ÈVE and ÊTE).

IÈRE is a familiar feminine ending and ÈVE is a VE ending and thus feminine. You've also met ÈGE before along with AGE as a masculine ending. The new ending that we encountered in this chapter is ÈRE. Nouns ending in ÈRE are fairly common and firmly mixed.

RULE THIRTY-FIVE

O-CONSONANT-E

Now let's go on to another group of nouns, those ending with O-CONSONANT-E.

Previously, you'll remember, we have found that the vowels U, I, or A preceding a CONSONANT-E ending indicate a feminine noun. For example: *facture, étude, crise, vitrine, fusillade* and *escale*.

I had every expectation that the vowel O preceding a CONSONANT-E ending would also indicate a feminine noun. In fact, I did find one O-CONSONANT-E noun ending that was feminine, the ending IOLE:

*Feminine nouns ending in **IOLE**: fiole luciole gloriole babiole carriole cabriole*

Unfortunately, that was the only one. The rest of the nouns ening in O-CONSONANT-E are mixed in gender and O-CONSONANT-E follows no rule.

Let's look at some of these endings. First we have the ending ODE, which is fairly common:

136

Nouns ending in ODE:

> *masculine: mode code nématode ixode épisode exode synode*

> *féminine: mode période commode ode méthode géode électrode anode cathode diode triode*

These are evidently mixed. Now the rest of the nouns ending in O-CONSONANT-E:

Other nouns ending in O-CONSONANT-E
> *(or Ô-CONSONANT-E):*

> *masculine: microbe éloge pétrole symbole contrôle rôle pôle môme tome idiome binôme diplôme axiome trombone téléphone cyclone télescope microscope magnétoscope héliotrope pore météore coyote azote vote gymnote hôte*

> *féminine: robe noce loge horloge rigole rougeole étole parole sole école idole casserole camisole boussole amazone matrone madone escalope chope aurore flore chose rose dextrose narcose névrose pelote litote gargote belote note capote paillote côte entrecôte boxe alcôve*

These are obviously mixed as well. This is therefore an easy rule:

Rule Thirty-Five

Nouns ending in either
O-CONSONANT-E or Ô-CONSONANT-E

are mixed and follow no rule (with the exception of IOLE).

Nouns ending in IOLE are feminine.

Rule Thirty-Six

RE

This brings us to those nouns ending in RE. As nouns ending in R are masculine, I rather expected those ending in RE to be feminine.

The first nouns of any frequency that I encountered with RE endings were the fairly common group ending in TRE. To my surprise, there seemed to be a predominance of masculine nouns in this group. It's almost enough to make it a masculine noun ending but there are enough common words which are feminine exceptions that you can't count on nouns in this group to follow a fixed rule. Let's look.

*Nouns ending in **TRE**:*

> masculine: *ventre pleutre semestre trimestre contre être pitre litre titre cadastre tertre monstre lustre rustre chapitre feutre maître traître âtre mètre manomètre centimètre pluviomètre désastre filtre centre épicentre spectre albâtre apôtre antre bellâtre*

> feminine: *huître vitre montre rencontre loutre martre*

lettre poutre fenêtre

I found that nouns ending in VRE were about evenly split:

*Nouns ending in **VRE**:*

> *masculine: livre givre lièvre poivre cadavre vivre*

> *feminine: lèvre chèvre fièvre manoeuvre pieuvre*
> *couleuvre oeuvre*

After that I thought back to some of the RE endings we had previously encountered and remembered that RRE was one of only two DOUBLE CONSONANT-E endings which was mixed instead of feminine (see Rule Seventeen):

*Nouns ending in **RRE**:*

> *masculine: cimeterre tonnerre verre lierre beurre parterre*

> *feminine: jarre bourre terre serre resserre escarre guerre*
> *Angleterre bagarre pierre barre amarre*

Feeling like a detective, I picked up the ORE and ÈRE noun endings from our last two rules of noun endings:

*Nouns ending in **ORE** and **ÈRE**:*

> *masculine: pore météore frère père hélicoptère monastère*
> *presbytère caractère mystère cerbère*
> *réverbère*

> *feminine: aurore congère patère bruyère galère artère*
> *bouchère boulangère misère étagère colère*
> *vipère enchère sphère atmosphère commère*
> *mère*

140

I added these endings to my growing collection of RE noun endings. So far, they were all mixed.

I remembered also that OIRE and ARE had been exceptions to the feminine rules Twenty-Eight and Twenty-Seven, and were also mixed noun endings:

*Nouns ending in **OIRE**:*

> *masculine: prétoire ivoire auditoire pourboire territoire Directoire conservatoire oratoire interrogatoire exutoire laboratoire accessoire*

> *feminine: échappatoire pétoire victoire passoire gloire nageoire mâchoire histoire armoire*

*Nouns ending in **ARE**:*

> *masculine: phare cigare*

> *feminine: tiare mare gare aérogare*

I accumulated a small group of additional RE noun endings which didn't seem to be either masculine or feminine or which didn't have enough examples to assign them to one or the other. These include the endings FRE, DRE, CRE, GRE, BRE, MRE NRE and YRE.

As a group these endings are predominantly masculine but unfortunately they have enough feminine exceptions that you cannot have confidence in assigning a new word masculine gender without checking it. We have to keep them in our group of noun endings which don't follow any rule.

*Nouns ending in **FRE, DRE, CRE, GRE, HRE, NRE, BRE**
and **YRE:***

*masculine: membre gingembre nombre timbre équilibre
sabre sacre diacre cancre massacre esclandre
cadre palissandre ordre désordre gendre
goinfre coffre chiffre bougre tigre congre
ogre camphre genre collyre*

*feminine: vertèbre chambre ombre encre ancre escadre
salamandre foudre poudre gaufre offre pègre*

As additional examples of these endings are identified, some could be designated as masculine endings, but as of now there isn't enough evidence to do so. For example, the finding of three masculine FRE words, *coffre, goinfre* and *chiffre*, and two feminine, *offre* and *gaufre*, doesn't allow us to do anything but assign FRE to the category of endings which do not follow any rule.

Finally, there are a few RE endings that we have previously encountered that are either masculine or feminine. IRE and its subgroup AIRE are masculine and URE and IÈRE are feminine.

*Masculine nouns ending in **IRE**: sbire sire cachemire empire
rire navire maire sourire délire
(exception: tirelire)*

*Masculine nouns ending in **AIRE**: formulaire éventaire
salaire sanctuaire exemplaire
dictionnaire luminaire documentaire
contraire anniversaire vestiaire*

repaire inventaire frigidaire
commentaire arbitraire ordinaire
militaire itinéraire annuaire
émissaire lampadaire rosaire calcaire
(exceptions: aire affaire grammaire
glaire circulaire)

Feminine nouns ending in **URE***: tenture mesure coiffure*
facture soudure ordure injure rayure
éraflure égratignure bravoure figure
rature mixture peinture allure heure
foulure blessure enflure brûlure
moisissure fissure capture garniture
levure lecture monture brochure
nature devanture désinvolture
morsure fracture tonsure salure
(exceptions: murmure parjure
cyanure)

Feminine nouns ending in **IÈRE***: matière glissière charnière*
muselière coursière tanière clairière
ornière visière infirmière épicière
paupière lumière rivière portière
manière crinière etc (exceptions:
cimetière derrière)

We can now conclude with:

Rule Thirty-Six

Nouns ending in RE are mixed and follow no rule, (with the exceptions of IRE and AIRE which are masculine and URE and IÈRE which are feminine).

URE and IÈRE are prominent feminine endings that we have encountered before. This will take some of the problem out of remembering these exceptions.

RULE THIRTY-SEVEN

Other Mixed Endings

Now we come to a few miscellaneous noun endings which we haven't seen before and which we can classify as mixed. Some may have relatively more examples of nouns of one sex or the other. However, as we mentioned before, an ending with twenty masculine endings and ten feminine still has to be classified as following no rule. This is because if you encountered a new noun with this ending, you couldn't assign it as either masculine or feminine with any confidence.

Here are five small miscellaneous groups of these mixed nouns:

*Nouns ending in **GLE** and **FLE**:*

> *masculine: souffle trèfle buffle girofle ongle aigle angle rectangle triangle seigle sigle*

> *feminine: pantoufle moufle gifle rafle tringle règle sangle épingle*

*Nouns ending in **STE**:*

> *masculine: faste contraste geste zeste inceste manifeste*

reste poste (telephone) arbuste kyste

feminine: peste veste liste piste mangouste poste (mail)

Nouns ending in LTE:

masculine: culte tumulte asphalte

feminine: insulte virevolte halte

Nouns ending in THE:

masculine: monolithe mégalithe aérolithe labyrinthe mythe

feminine: plinthe absinthe berthe

Among nouns ending in THE is the word *psychopathe* which can be masculine or feminine according to the subject.

These, of course, are fairly small groups, so the rule is not one of our most important ones.

Rule Thirty-Seven

Nouns ending in GLE, FLE, STE, LTE and THE are mixed.

RULE THIRTY-EIGHT

PHE

PHE was listed in the early editions as an orphan ending because I didn't have enough examples to give it a home as either a masculine, a feminine or a mixed ending. It is now turning out to be an unusual ending, divided into words ending in RAPHE and (G)RAPHE, which are masculine, and those ending in TROPHE and YMPHE which are feminine.

For the **RAPHE** and **GRAPHE** endings I have found nine **masculine** examples and just one exception:

> *paraphe graphe paragraphe phonographe*
> *autographe télégraphe piézographe*
> *électrocardiographe dactylographe* (machine)

> *(exception: orthographe)*

In addition we have three words which can be masculine or feminine depending on the person being talked about. These will be obvious from context:

stenographe dactylographe (person)
photographe

I have found one **TAPHE** ending, *épitaphe*, which, oddly enough, is feminine.

I have found three examples of words ending in **TROPHE**. They are all feminine:

strophe catastrophe apostrophe

and two ending in **YMPHE**, which are also all feminine.

nymphe lymphe

Please take into account that the TROPHE and YMPHE endings have only a few examples at present and their status could change.

Rule Thirty-Eight

Nouns ending in PHE are divided into those ending in RAPHE and GRAPHE which are masculine, and those ending in TROPHE and YMPHE which seem to be feminine.

Review of Mixed Endings Which We Have Encountered Previously as Exceptions to Other Rules

You will remember that in going through our masculine and feminine noun endings we came across several sub-groups which were exceptions to those rules and were mixed endings.

We will review these mixed endings which were exceptions to other rules now, to help you to group them in your mind with the rest of the mixed noun endings we've just discussed.

*Nouns ending in **MME**:*

> *masculine:* dilemme parallélogramme homme ncéphalogramme programme télégramme idéogramme somme *(nap)*

> *feminine:* femme pomme gamme somme *(sum)* flamme flemme tomme gemme

*Nouns ending in **RRE**:*

> *masculine:* cimeterre tonnerre verre lierre beurre parterre

> *feminine:* bourre jarre terre serre resserre escarre guerre Angleterre bagarre pierre barre amarre erre

*Nouns ending in **ICE** which are not female occupations:*

   masculine: bénéfice exercice appendice service délice
                artifice caprice indice orifice

   feminine: hélice malice matrice police épice nourrice

*Nouns ending in **GUE**:*

   masculine: gringue exergue pirogue bouledogue orgue

   feminine: dague fugue longue mangue langue bague
               blague fatigue drogue morgue seringue
               fougue ligue

*Nouns ending in **QUE**:*

   masculine: kiosque risque phoque masque casque disque
                manque chèque roque

   feminine: casaque laque loque equivoque banque claque
               planque cloque bicoque bourrasque vasque
               marque barque bisque époque matraque
               pastèque attaque toque hypothèque coque

*Nouns ending in **IQUE**:*

   masculine: classique moustique pique-nique Mexique
                diurétique pique (spade suit)

   feminine: mystique (mysticism) botanique brique Belgique
               Jamaïque musique critique (criticism)
               boutique logique Amérique panique
               politique fabrique république bique pique
               (pike)

masculine or feminine depending on the person: critique mystique

Nouns ending in **IDE:**

    masculine: bolide liquide fluide fongicide insectide vide homicide génocide bide

    feminine: aide (help) ride pyramide égide

Nouns ending in **IFE:**

    masculine: calife

Nouns ending in **IGE:**

    masculine: prestige vertige vestige

    feminine: égide neige tige

Nouns ending in **ILE:**

    masculine: volatile mobile asile domicile bile vigile fossile crocodile voile (veil)

    feminine: étoile voile (sail) toile aile argile île

Nouns ending in **IME:**

    masculine: régime abîme crime millésime

    feminine: escrime rime prime frime déprime victime lime cime

Nouns ending in **IPE:**

    masculine: principe

feminine: pipe équipe

*Nouns ending in **ITE**:*

    masculine: termite satellite ermite site rite granite graphite anthracite trilobite plébiscite mérite

    feminine: mite fuite réussite poursuite suite marmite dynamite hépatite bronchite orbite appendicite

*Nouns ending in **IXE**:*

    masculine: préfixe fixe

    feminine: rixe

*Nouns ending in **STE**:*

    masculine: faste geste reste poste (telephone, etc) *arbuste kyste*

    feminine: peste veste liste piste poste (mail)

*Nouns ending in **UBE, UGE, UCE** and **UME**:*

    masculine: incube succube cube tube grabuge ignifuge subterfuge juge pouce costume chaume volume royaume rhume

    feminine: aube puce jauge sauge luge auge brume plume paume

*Nouns ending in **ASE, ARE, AZE** and **AKE**:*

    masculine: vase (for flowers) *phare cigare kamikaze*

feminine: vase (*mud*) base phrase tiare mare gaze cake

Nouns ending in Â-CONSONANT-E

 masculine: râle mâle crâne âne châle blâme

 feminine: râpe âme

Observation on TE endings

In previous editions I had presented TE as a feminine ending. However as I researched this fourth edition it became clear that the situation was so complicated that it made sense to eliminate TE as a separate rule altogether. Let me explain why.

Some TE endings are indeed **feminine**. You are familiar with **TTE** words *(assiette, chatte).* There are lots of them and they're just about all feminine.

You also have encountered **NTE** and **RTE** in our rules for N- and R-CONSONANT-T endings. These are also feminine *(la patiente, la plainte, la carte).*

However, when we continue with other consonants before the TE ending, we come to the endings **CTE**, **HTE**, **PTE**, and **XTE**. These are all <u>masculine</u> *(un insecte, le compte, le contexte, etc)*, although there aren't many examples to go on.

It gets worse! Nouns ending with **STE** and **LTE** are <u>mixed</u> and don't follow any rule at all *(le geste, la peste* and *un culte, une insulte).*

Also remember that nouns ending in **ISTE** and referring to a person, like *cycliste* and *socialiste* can be <u>masculine or feminine</u> depending on the person referred to.

We discovered that **UTE** and **ATE** are feminine endings when we looked at U- and A-CONSONANT-E endings. **ÈTE** and **ÊTE** lean feminine as well, although the samples are small.

However, we also learned that **ITE** and **OTE** are <u>mixed</u> when we discussed I- and O-CONSONSANT-E endings.

As you can see, TE endings are really a mess. And you can't be expected to remember each little ending!

It's a good idea remember that the common noun endings TTE, UTE, RTE and NTE are feminine, but you don't have to remember them as "TE endings". They are all examples of other feminine rules that we've already encountered: the DOUBLE-CONSONANT-E rule, and the U, R, and N-CONSONANT-E rules.

You also know the masculine endings CTE, PTE and XTE from Rule Thirteen, and we've covered all the rest of the TE endings in other rules. Thus TE is one less rule to worry about.

Words for People

This chapter doesn't give you an additional Rule. It's rather to discuss some of the odd ways that the French language deals with words for people.

Think of it this way: A chair is always _une chaise_ and courage is always _le courage_, but people (and animals) come in two sexes. They can be masculine or feminine. This adds a certain complexity and the language has to decide what to do about it.

There are different possible ways to deal with this "complication":

> You can use the **same** noun and **same** gender irrespective of whether the person involved is a man or a woman (_une victime,_ for example).

> You can use the **same** noun all the time but **vary** the gender (_un enfant_ and _une enfant_).

> You can change **both** the noun **and** the gender depending on whether you are talking about a man or a woman _(un menteur_ and _une menteuse)._

As you have just seen, rather than choosing one of these three methods, French has chosen to use all three (for different nouns). There are thus three different kinds of people nouns.

1. – The first group of nouns are truly invariable. You use the **same** noun and the **same** gender irrespective of whether you are talking about a man or a woman.

In other words, each of these nouns is either <u>always masculine or always feminine</u>, no matter the sex of the person that it refers to.

For example, *la victime* and *la canaille* are **always** feminine even if the victim or the scoundrel is a man, and *le sosie* is always masculine, even if *le sosie* happens to be a woman.

Here are a few sample nouns from this category, just to familiarize you with them. There are many, many more. Most nouns in this group will turn out to be masculine as they are the name of what used to be exclusively masculine occupations.

Nouns which are either always masculine or always feminine:

Masculine: un plombier, un médecin, un professeur, un génie, un sosie, un chef

Feminine: une victime, une personne, une crapule, une sentinelle, une canaille

You can thus have such odd sentences as <u>Pierre</u> est <u>la</u> victime, <u>Robert</u> est <u>une</u> vraie crapule, <u>Mireille</u> se prend pour <u>un</u> génie, <u>Gérard</u> est <u>la</u> sentinelle, and <u>Colette</u> est <u>le</u> sosie de Mireille.

2. – The second group of nouns are also invariable. They don't change their form in talking about a man or a woman. However, these nouns, while not changing form, **do** change their gender. They become <u>either masculine or feminine depending on who you are referring to.</u>

For example: _Pierre_ est _un_ enfant and _Colette_ est _une_ enfant, _un_ collègue and _une_ collègue, _le_ comptable and _la_ comptable, or _un_ élève and _une_ élève.

Note again that the noun **doesn't** change form as it changes from masculine to feminine. In other words, _"enfant"_ doesn't change, or take an _–e._ It just changes gender.

Here's a very partial list. I'm giving you these just as examples of what I'm talking about. (There are hundreds more).

> _**Nouns which can be either masculine or feminine (without changing form):** enfant comptable collègue élève môme gosse dentiste pianiste communiste millionaire fonctionnaire critique mystique lâche somnambule aide guide imbécile interprète maniaque_

3. – There is a third group of people names in which the noun is variable. In other words, you use a <u>different noun, with a different gender</u>, depending on whether you are talking about a man or a woman .

This group includes nouns such as _gamin_ which simply adds an _-e_ to become _gamine,_ and others like _un acteur_ which changes its ending entirely to become _une actrice,_ and many other varieties. Here are a few examples:

> **Nouns that have different forms for masculine or feminine:**

> _acteur-actrice, boulanger-boulangère, électricien-électricienne, gamin-gamine, ennemi-ennemie menteur-menteuse danseur-danseuse épicier-épicière_

Current usage: Language is a fluid thing, and words for what used to be male occupations are slipping from the first group to the second group.

For example, most dictionaries will list *professeur* and *chef* as masculine words, and twenty years ago they always were, even if you were talking about a woman. However, in practice, many people now say *la professeur* and *la chef* when talking about a woman, and do the same for most occupational words.

Both forms are acceptable *(le professeur* and *la professeur,* for example). I recently encountered the expression *la professeur de dessin* in a novel by an author who writes in very elegant French. Be aware however that you may encounter language purists who still insist that it's always *le professeur.*

In Canada you may see *la professeure* (with an –e at the end) but this form would definitely not be accepted in France.

Chirurgien, on the other hand, is sliding from the first group to the third group. You can treat it as an invariable noun and say *Elle va être le chirurgien,* or you can treat it as a noun which changes according to the sex and say *Elle va être la chirurgienne.* Both are apparently acceptable.

Animals: Most animal and bird names fit into the first group. They are always masculine or always feminine regardless of the sex of the animal. For example *un rat* is *un rat* whether it is a male or female rat, and *une taupe* is *une taupe* regardless of it's sex. Here are a few examples:

Masculine: un rat, un oiseau, un animal, un leopard, un tigre

Feminine: une souris, une taupe, une hirondelle

For some animals, however, there is a different French name for the male and the female. Consider: *le chien* and *la chienne*, *le chat* and *la chatte*, *un lion* and *une lionne*, *une vache* and *un taureau*.

The good news is that, with all these nouns dealing with people (and animals), those which are always masculine or always feminine generally follow our rules for gender so that when you encounter one of them you'll know if it's a masculine or feminine noun. For example, *médecin, plombier, professeur* and *taureau* all have masculine endings. *Personne*, with its NNE ending is clearly feminine, as is *taupe*, with a UPE ending and *vache* with a CHE ending.

In addition, when there is a different name for male and female people, occupations or animals, they also follow our male and female ending rules. Think of *acteur* and *actrice*, *menteur* and *menteuse*, *électricien* and *électricienne*, *chat* and *chatte*, *vache* and *taureau*, etc.

Conclusion

Now that you have come to the end of this study you probably realize better than when you started that it is a work in process. While some of the common endings are very clearly either masculine or feminine, there are other endings listed as masculine, feminine or mixed for which there really aren't enough examples yet to be completely sure. These endings could possibly change their place in a future edition. Some, indeed, have changed for this Fourth Edition.

There are other endings for which I have not yet found a home. For example, In an earlier edition I remarked that I had found only one example of a THE ending, which didn't allow me to place it in any category. Friends found several more examples for me and now you will find it in Rule Thirty-Seven among the miscellaneous endings which are mixed.

PHE was listed as another orphan ending In those earlier editions but you will now find it discussed in Rule Thirty-Eight.

On the other hand other endings like LME and LBE are still orphans. As of now I have only two examples of an LME ending, one masculine, one feminine *(calme palme),* and just one for LBE *(le galbe).* Neither of these endings belong to any larger family of endings so for now there is no good place to classify them. As other examples turn up, they may find more definitive homes.

I include these examples of changes in progress to help you understand the real empirical nature of a study like this as well as the reasoning that goes into it. It's important to realize that you shouldn't consider these rules as hard and fast, but as guides.

If you are in a conversation and you come to a noun and don't know whether to say *le* or *la*, or to describe it as *blanc* or *blanche*, or *fort* or *forte*, these rules will give you a very good guess. "Oh yes, it ends in *ment* so it's masculine" or "it ends in *elle* so it's feminine". However, if it's an ending with exceptions, and it's your end-of-term paper and it's got to be correct, look it up!

In conclusion, I hope that you have found this study as fascinating as I have.

List of Rules

Rules for Masculine Nouns

Rule One

Nouns ending in T are masculine.

Rule Two

Singular nouns ending in S are masculine.

Rule Three

Nouns ending in C are masculine.

Rule Four

Nouns ending in I and Y are masculine.

Rule Five

Nouns ending in U are masculine.

Rule Six

Nouns ending in L are masculine.

Rule Seven

Nouns ending in D are masculine.

Rule Eight

Nouns ending in N are masculine with the exception of those ending in ION, ISON and ISSON, all of which tend to be feminine.

Note especially that the common endings TION, SION and AISON are almost always feminine.

Rule Nine

Nouns ending in R (with the exception of EUR) are masculine.

Nouns ending in EUR that refer to a person or thing that does something are also masculine.

The rest of the EUR nouns are feminine.

Rule Ten

Nouns ending in other consonants are also masculine with the exception of those ending in OIX.

Nouns ending in OIX are predominantly feminine.

Rule Eleven

Nouns ending in O are masculine.

Rule Twelve

Nouns ending in A are masculine, with the exception of those imported from Italian or Spanish.

Rule Thirteen

The following noun endings are masculine, in spite of ending in E:

AGE and ÈGE
IRE (IRE and AIRE)
SME (ISME, ASME, OSME, YSME)
Other ME endings: THME, GME and NYME
CLE, BLE and PLE
CTE, HTE, PTE and XTE
TYPE
XE and ZE

Rule Fourteen

Nouns ending in É are masculine, (with the exception of those ending in IÉ and TÉ).

Nouns ending in TÉ are feminine, while those ending in IÉ are mixed.

Rule Fifteen

Most compound nouns are masculine, irrespective of their noun endings, especially the important groups starting with PARA, PARE, ANTI, GARDE, PORTE, CASSE, ESSUIE and others.

Rules for Feminine Nouns

Rule Sixteen - Feminine nouns not ending in E:

Nouns ending in ISON and ISSON tend to be feminine. The important group ending in AISON is feminine with no exceptions.

Nouns ending in ION are feminine with the exception of the small groups ending in PION and LION.

Nouns ending in EUR, that do <u>not</u> refer to a person or a thing that does something, are feminine.

Rule Seventeen

Nouns ending in a double consonant followed by E are feminine (with the exception of MME and RRE).

Nouns ending in MME and RRE are mixed.

Rule Eighteen

Nouns ending ÉE are feminine.

Rule Nineteen

Nouns with the classic feminine endings EUSE, IÈRE, IENNE and TRICE are indeed feminine.

Rule Twenty

Nouns with ANCE, ENCE, and other NCE and NSE endings, are feminine.

Rule Twenty-One

Nouns ending with IE are feminine.

The few ending in IÉ are mixed and follow no rule.

Rule Twenty-Two

Nouns ending with UE are feminine (with the exception of GUE and QUE).

Nous ending in GUE and QUE are mixed.

Rule Twenty-Three

Nouns ending with CHE are feminine

Rule Twenty-Four

Nouns ending with MPE and MBE are feminine

Rule Twenty-Five

Nouns ending with TÉ are feminine.

Note especially the very common ending ITÉ

Rule Twenty-Six

Nouns ending in U-CONSONANT-E are predominantly feminine, but some less common subgroups are mixed.

Rule Twenty-Seven

Nouns ending in A-CONSONANT-E (with the exception of AGE) are predominantly feminine.

Nouns ending in AGE are masculine.

Rule Twenty-Eight

The I-CONSONANT-E endings are a mess.

The common endings IVE, ISE, INE, A̲INE, and TRICE are feminine.

IRE and A̲IRE are masculine!

Other I-CONSONANT-E endings, including the important endings OIRE, ICE and ITE, are mixed and follow no rule.

Rule Twenty-Nine

Nouns ending in R-CONSONANT-E are mostly feminine (with the exception of those ending in RRE).

Nouns ending in RRE are mixed.

Rule Thirty

Nouns ending in N-CONSONANT-E are feminine with the exception of NGE which is mixed.

Rule Thirty-One

Nouns ending in VE are feminine.

Rule Thirty-Two

Nouns ending with GNE are predominantly feminine.

Rule Thirty-Three

Wines, trees, colors, numbers, days of the
week, months, and seasons are masculine.

Autos are feminine, and the genders of
nouns in other categories are determined
in a similar fashion when the nouns don't
stand alone but are "abbreviations".

For example when _une_ Renault means _une_
voiture Renault, or _un_ chèvre means _un_
fromage de chèvre.

Rules for Mixed Endings

Rule Thirty-Four

Nouns ending in È-CONSONANT-E and
Ê-CONSONANT-E are mixed and follow no
rule (with the exception of the masculine
ending ÈGE, and the feminine endings
IÈRE, ÈVE and ÊTE).

Rule Thirty-Five

Nouns ending in either O-CONSONANT-E or
Ô-CONSONANT-E are mixed and follow no
rule (with the exception of IOLE).

Nouns ending in IOLE are feminine.

Rule Thirty-Six

Nouns ending in RE are mixed and follow
no rule, (with the exceptions of IRE and
AIRE which are masculine and URE and

IÈRE which are feminine).

Rule Thirty-Seven

Nouns ending in GLE, FLE, STE, LTE and THE are mixed.

Rule Thirty-Eight

Nouns ending in PHE are divided into those ending in RAPHE and GRAPHE which are masculine, and those ending in TROPHE and YMPHE which seem to be feminine.

Index of Noun Endings

Since this is an index arranged alphabetically by noun ENDINGS and NOT alphabetically by the BEGINNINGS of words as we are used to, we have to work from the end of the word backwards.

Thus to find a noun ending in this index, start at the terminal letter and work backwards. For example, if you are looking up the ending of the word *fenouil,* go down the alphabet **by terminal letter** until you arrive at L, then look down past AL and EL until you come to IL, continue on down to UIL, and finally arrive at OUIL. Go ahead and try it now to be sure that you understand.

(It's the exact opposite of a normal alphabetizing where to find the same word you have to first find F, then FE, then FEN and FENO, etc.)

Similarly, for example, the ending PE will come before RE , because P comes before R. The endings ARE and then IRE will be found below RE, while AIRE and OIRE are found below IRE.

A letter with an accent will follow the same letter without the accent. Thus, a word ending in É will come after ALL the E endings.

172

ÈME	34	CRE	36
ÊME	34	DRE	36
GME	13	ÈRE	34, 36
THME	13	IÈRE	19, 34, 36
IME	28	FRE	36
MME	17	GRE	36
LME	Conc.	HRE	36
OME	35	IRE	13, 26, 28, 36
RME	29	AIRE	13, 28, 36
ASME	13	OIRE	28, 36
ISME	13	NRE	36
OSME	13	ORE	26, 35, 36
YSME	13	RRE	17, 29, 36
UME	26	TRE	36
NYME	13	URE	26, 36
ANE	27	AURE	26
ÈNE	34	VRE	36
ÊNE	34	YRE	36
GNE	32	ASE	27
INE	26, 28	ÈSE	34
AINE	28	ISE	28
EINE	28	AISE	28
OINE	28	OISE	28
UINE	28	NSE	20, 30
UNE	26	ANSE	20, 30
NNE	17, 30	ENSE	20
ANNE	17	ONSE	20
ENNE	17	OSE	35
IENNE	17, 19	RSE	29
ONNE	17	SSE	17
ONE	35	ASSE	17
RNE	29	ESSE	17
UNE	26	ISSE	17
APE	27	OSSE	17
ÈPE	34	USSE	17
IPE	28	YSSE	17
MPE	24	USE	26
OPE	35	EUSE	19, 26
PPE	17	OUSE	26
RPE	29	TE	Observ on TE
UPE	26	ATE	27
TYPE	13	CTE	13
RE	26, 36	ÊTE	34
ARE	26, 27, 36	ÈTE	34
BRE	36	HTE	13

ITE	28	RTÉ	25
LTE	37	AUTÉ	25
OTE	35	F	10
MTE	13	G	10
NTE	30	H	10
PTE	13	I	4
RTE	29	AI	4
STE	13, 37	BI	4
ISTE	13	CI	4
TTE	17	DI	4
ATTE	17	FI	4
ETTE	17	HI	4
ITTE	17	KI	4
OTTE	17	LI	4
UTTE	17	MI	4
UTE	26	NI	4
XTE	13	OI	4, 10
UE	22	PI	4
GUE	22	RI	4
OUE	22	SI	4
QUE	22	TI	4
IQUE	22	UI	4
VE	31	WI	4
AVE	27, 31	XI	4
ÈVE	31, 34	ZI	4
ÊVE	31, 34	K	10
IVE	28, 31	L	6
LVE	31	AL	6
ÔVE	31	EL	6
RVE	29, 31	IL	6
UVE	26, 31	AIL	6
XE	13	EIL	6
IXE	28	OIL	6
YE	21	UIL	6
ZE	13	EUIL	6
IZE	28	OUIL	6
É	14	OL	6
IÉ	14, 21	UL	6
TÉ	14, 25	M	10
ETÉ	25	N	8
ÉTÉ	25	AN	8
ITÉ	25	EN	8
LTÉ	25	IEN	8
NTÉ	25	IN	8
PTÉ	25	AIN	8

174

EIN	8	NS	2
OIN	8	OS	2
OUIN	8	PS	2
ON	8	RS	2
ION	8, 16	OURS	2
CION	8, 16	TS	2
FION	16	US	2
GION	8, 16	OUS	2
LION	16	YS	2
MION	16	T	1
NION	8, 16	AT	1
PION	16	CT	1
SION	8, 16	ET	1
TION	8, 16	IT	1
VION	16	OIT	1
XION	8, 16	GT	1
ISON	8, 16	NT	1
AISON	8, 16	ANT	1
OISON	8, 16	ENT	1
ISSON	8, 16	MENT	1
OISSON	8,16	INT	1
O	11	OINT	1
P	10	ONT	1
Q	10	OT	1
R	9	PT	1
AR	9	RT	1
ER	9	ST	1
IER	9	TT	1
IR	9	UT	1
AIR	9	U	5
OIR	9	AU	5
OR	9	EAU	5
UR	9	RAU	5
YR	9	YAU	5
EUR	9, 16	EU	5
OUR	9	OU	5
S	2	X	10
AS	2	OIX	10
DS	2	EUX	10
ES	2	Y	4
ÈS	2	W	10
IS	2	Z	10
AIS	2		
OIS	2		
LS	2		

Boiling it all down!

This is a distillation of the most useful endings, those which are both common and either overwhelmingly masculine or overwhelmingly feminine. I'm giving them to you in broad brushstrokes. This means I'm ignoring small exceptions. I'm also not mentioning here many other masculine and feminine endings which are either less common or less consistent, and which you'll find in the text. This is the "Big Picture".

Masculine endings

Let's summarize what we have learned about masculine endings.

1. - Nouns ending in <u>any</u> consonant are reliably masculine with three exceptions: N, R and X.

> **For the N endings**, the big common exceptions are words ending in AISON, TION and SION *(la maison, la population, la conclusion, etc)*. (There are other exceptions of course).

> **For the R endings**, the exceptions are those ending in EUR but not referring to someone or something that does something *(la candeur, la chaleur, etc)*.

> **For the X endings**, the exceptions are words ending in OIX *(la voix, etc)*.

2. - **Nouns ending in the vowels I, O, and U are reliably masculine** *(le souci, le mémento, le veto, le menu, le clou, etc).*

> **Nouns ending in the vowel A** are masculine with the exception of those words imported from Italian or Spanish *(la pizza, la mafia, la polenta, etc).*

3. - **Among nouns ending in E, the common endings AGE, ÈGE** *(le courage, le piège),* **ISME, ASME** *(le capitalisme, le sarcasme)* **IRE, AIRE** *(le sourire, le formulaire),* **CLE, BLE and PLE** *(le miracle, le possible, le peuple)* **are masculine. É is also masculine** *(le marché),* **but not** when it's a **TÉ** *(la santé, la fraternité).*

4. - **Wines, trees, numbers, colors, months, seasons, days of the week, and compound words, are masculine** *(un bourgogne, le saule, un mille, un rouge clair, un septembre affreux, un été merveilleux, le dimanche, le pare-brise).*

Feminine endings

Feminine endings are a lot less clear and have more exceptions. I'll include only the most common and reliable.

1. - **LLE, NNE, SSE, TTE, FFE and PPE are reliably feminine** *(mademoiselle, patronne, tendresse, fourchette, gaffe, nappe).*

> On the other hand, MME and RRE are mixed *(une femme, un homme, la pierre, le verre).*

2. - **The common endings ÉE, IE, CHE, VE, NCE, EUSE, IÉRE, TRICE and TÉ** (especially ITÉ) **are feminine** *(la soirée, la maladie, la bouche, la cave, la confiance, la conférence, la danseuse, la lumière, une actrice, la santé, la fraternité).*

3. - **The common endings URE, UDE** *(la mesure, la solitude),* **ADE** *(la façade),* **ISE, AISE, INE, AINE** *(la crise, la chaise,* *la colline, la fontaine)*, **NTE, NDE** *(la descente, la bande)* **and GNE** *(la vigne)* **are also feminine.**

4. – Nouns ending in R-consonant-E are feminine, no matter what the consonant *(la ferme, la force, la porte, la bourse).*